UNCOMMON
Life

SAFECRACKER CHRONICLES

LUCIOUS DALE JOHNSON

Uncommon Life

Copyright © 2019 by Lucious Dale Johnson. All rights reserved.

No part of this book may be reproduced or transmitted in any form or by any means, electronic or mechanical, including photocopying, recording, or by any information storage and retrieval system, without the express written permission of the author.

ISBN-13: 978-1-6940623-6-9

Facebook: facebook.com/ScreenwriterOrg
Twitter: @ScreenwriterOrg
Medium: medium.com/@wideview00

I dedicate this book to my mother, Celia Johnson. Thank you for my life. And to my fiancée, Snizhana Koval, for our great relationship. I would also like to thank Screenwriting Partners for their story services.

UNCOMMON *Life*

PART I

AN UNCOMMON LIFE

It all started at West Palm Beach, Florida, the place I was born. We lived there for a few years then moved to Ft. Walton Beach, Florida. I was living with my mother, my father, my loving sister, and my brother. Our home was on a large piece of land, and we had four bedrooms, a front porch, and a big fishpond out back. We also had two goats. We would attach them to a wagon and drive around the neighborhood. It was cool.

My father's name was Lucious Daniel Johnson. He was born in Florida, too, and passed away in 1982 at the age of fifty-two. My sister's name was Linda Diane Johnson. We lost her in 1960. My mother's name was Celia Constance Johnson. She was still living with me in Pennsylvania until she passed away in December 2011. She was eighty-four. God bless them. My brother's name is Lynn Dale Johnson. He was born in 1957—still with us.

My father was an entrepreneur. He owned a roofing company, a chain-link fence company, and a bar called The Reef Inn. He was also a pro boxer and a heavy drinker. His fight name was Kid Johnson, and sometimes, he broke out of the normal life and did out of the norm things. Like one time….

THE TOY GUN

My father was a hard worker, but like I said, a hard drinker. I remember a few unusual things that happened when he drank. One time, he took my toy machine gun—which shot out flames and sounded like a real weapon—down to the bar my family owned, and he took me with him. I was just a young boy, and I felt awfully lucky at the time.

It was about 8:00 p.m. on a rainy night. We pulled into the back of the bar. The parking lot had enormous potholes in it. He knew that a few people from the bar gathered out back to smoke. He was right. There were three men and three women. My father jumped out of the car and yelled, "I'm going to kill you all!" and then started firing away.

They all tried to rush in the back door, which opened out, jamming six people in the doorway. One man tried to climb into the big, heavy-duty outdoor icebox. One of the women decided to run around to the front door, but she fell in a mud puddle. The other two women were yelling, "Lou's gonna kill us all!"

That's when my father stopped shooting and yelled, "It's only a toy gun."

He then went to the woman that fell and helped her up. Everyone came over to look at the toy gun. They were pissed off. Plus, everyone was coming outside and around the back to see what was going on.

My father yelled, "It's okay. Drinks are on me!"

So, we headed into the bar and grabbed some towels for the muddy woman. After they all had some drinks in them, they were laughing about the whole thing. Everyone wanted to kill my father, but they knew he was no one to fuck with.

HERE COMES THE SHERIFF

A few months after the fake shooting, my father and I were down at The Reef Inn, cleaning up after a week of people drinking. The sheriff stopped by. He told my dad that he heard he had a handgun in the bar. Naturally, knowing who my father was, the sheriff wanted to get the handgun.

My dad pulled out the gun and asked the sheriff if it was the one he was looking for.

The sheriff backed up a little and said, "Lou,"—everyone that knew my father called him Lou—"I do not want any trouble out of you."

My father then told him that we were going to close the bar, and he started turning off all the lights.

The sheriff said, "Come on, Lou, do not start with me."

My father asked him, "Who told you about the gun?"

He said, "You know I can't tell you that."

My father walked around the counter of the bar, where the sheriff and I were sitting. The sheriff then started to back out of the bar with his hand on his gun. I thought this was very cool. I felt like I was in some kind of cowboy movie from the fifties. While the sheriff was backing away, my father was moving steadily forward. Now, I must tell you that my father never pointed his gun at the sheriff.

I'll never know if the sheriff wasn't pulling his gun because of me, or because my father was not a treacherous man. Anyway, we made it outside the bar.

The sheriff said, "Come on, Lou, give me the gun."

My father told me to get in the car as he walked to the driver's side, and we got in. I heard the sheriff say, "Oh shit!"

We started up the car, and I thought Dad would go 100 miles per hour out of that place. To my surprise, we did like the O.J. Simpson Bronco chase and moved out of there nice and easy. We went right on the main road at five miles per hour. The sheriff's car was right behind us with the lights on, siren blasting, and the sheriff on the loudspeaker yelling, "Lou, stop!"

The road was backing up because of how slow we were going. So, after a few minutes of this breakneck speed, my father pulled into a bank and stopped. He climbed out and put the gun on the roof of the car, walked around to the front, and put his hands on the hood.

The sheriff got out of his car and put handcuffs on my father, and then another sheriff's car came. He escorted me out of my father's car and put me in his patrol car. The other sheriff put Dad in the other vehicle. The sheriff got in the car I was in and drove me home.

Once we got to my house, they told my mother what was going on. Now, my mother was the smart one. She called her friend to come over to watch us. A few hours later, Dad was home. We never talked about this again.

PLAYING INDIANS

Near where we lived was a horse stable. We'd walk across the road and go two blocks up to a plot of federal land behind the stable.

That's where I'd played since I was six years old. We were living like a normal family, for the most part. I guess seeing my father act wild and against social expectations made me curious about both sides of life, good and bad.

Not long after Father's police chase incident, a friend and I were out on the federal land playing Indians. We were shooting our arrows around for about a half hour or so. Then, I decided to do like the Indians do on TV—wrap dry leaves around my arrows, start them on fire, and shoot them into the woods. So, we did that. We shot about six to ten arrows that way.

When the woods caught fire, we got the hell out of there. As we were running, I instructed my friend not to tell anyone. He promised he wouldn't. I flew to my house, and he went to his.

A few days passed by, and then a federal officer showed up at my house. First, he talked to my mother, and then my mother called me into the living room. I sat down, and my mother told me I better tell him the truth. Then, he informed me that someone was up in the woods and started a fire a few days ago that burned a few thousand acres of land. He asked me if I was the one who started the fire in the woods.

I told him, "No."

He asked, "Are you sure about that?"

I reiterated that I wasn't the one who did it. When he asked if I knew who started the blaze, I simply said, "No."

He said, "That's all I needed," and advised that if I found anything out to tell my mother. She had his phone number.

I said, "Okay," and went back outside to play.

That was the last time I remember seeing him, and nothing ever came up about that fire again. A few days after that, I journeyed to my friend's house and asked him what happened. He told me that someone at the stables saw us running that day. I asked him if he admitted anything to that man or the federal officer. He said, "No."

Neither of us heard anything ever again about the fire or saw that officer.

I learned two things with that experience: never rat on yourself, and never do anything with anyone who is not a hundred percenter.

FINDING TREASURE

Another friend of mine lived behind the bar with his family in a small house. Across the street, there were two square miles of sand dunes. One day, we were playing out in front of his house when one of us had the bright idea to sift through the dunes to search for buried treasures.

We sat down to figure out how we were going to do this. His dad was a junk collector. So, we came up with the idea to get some door screen and nail it to some wood so that we could sift lots of sand at one time. We walked around his house, hunting for the materials, and, as luck would have it, there they were—some window screens with light metal frames. We took two and headed to the dunes.

After about a half hour of running around and stopping here and there at different dunes, we decided to focus on one spot. After sifting sand for about ten minutes, a handful of coins appeared. We could not believe our eyes. We sat there for a while, admiring the coins. My friend picked one up, and then I picked one up. We finally put the coins in our pockets and started to dig for more. After nearly an hour of not finding any more coins, we went back to his house.

His father was standing there. We told him what happened, and we showed him our coins. We had about ten. He was a little dumbfounded with what we found. They were gold coins. He wanted to know what sand dune we had dug these coins from. We mentioned the upper half of the beach. When we were done, I put them back in my pocket.

I walked home and showed my mother and father the coins. We didn't know what we had, so we took them to a coin dealer. He advised us we had genuine gold coins, and two of them had the head of Caesar on them. The dealer didn't have any books on them and asked Dad if he would leave the coins so he could find out more. So, Dad left the coins and told the man he'd be back in two weeks. The dealer told my dad that was fine. We walked back to the car and went home.

About a month passed by, and my father stopped back at the coin dealer. He told my father he could not find out anything on the coins because they were ancient and confirmed that it really was Caesar on the two of them. Dad brought the coins back to the house and put them in his drawer.

A few weeks later, I snuck into his room and took out the coins to show and tell at my school. It is fair to say the coins were a big hit. So, after school, the big kids wanted to play with me. But, what I didn't know was that by the end of the day, my coins would be missing.

One more lesson to learn: do not trust anyone. When I got home, I explained to my father what happened. We went to all the kids' homes to no avail—no coins. My father was so mad he beat me bad.

LOSING MY HEART

Everything was okay for a few years after the fire and buried treasure. When I was eight, we had a great, big backyard, and one day, Mom was burning the trash in a fifty-five gallon can. My sister and I were playing around the can when something popped and my sister's pants caught on fire. I ran and found my mother. She came running and put the fire out, but by then my sister's leg was badly burned. Mom called the ambulance, and they came and took my sister to the hospital.

While my sister, who was only ten at the time, was in the hospital for her burns, they discovered that she had a brain tumor. They gave her about six months to live. My mother and father took her to a few different hospitals around the United States, but, about ten months later, my sister died in our home on the couch.

That changed our lives forever. Life kicked us hard when she passed on. My mother tried so hard to save her that, in the end, my parents had lost everything—the fence company, the bar, the roofing company, and then the house. Our lives would never be the same.

MOVING TO READING

In 1962, we packed up what we had left and moved to Reading, Pennsylvania, where my mother was from. Her family was still there. We moved into a two-story apartment at 3rd and Walnut. Everything was hard for us. My father could not find any work, mostly because he talked with a Southern accent. It was a tremendous change for all of us. But life must go on.

My school was about half a block away. I was ten years old and coming into my own the very first time I saw a violent act against another human being. I saw my first fight. It was between two teenage boys. I didn't know what it was about, but they squared off and got right into it. The first one to throw a punch got the other guy right in the throat—a winning shot. The other teen was done.

I learned another life lesson: the first rule of war is that there are no rules. I went home knowing I would have done the same thing.

SEX ED

My first sex lesson was watching through the heat vent at home. My father was doing my mother. What a sight. I thought it was pretty funny, and I was laughing so hard my father heard me. I must have messed up his groove. He came upstairs mad as hell, but he just looked at me. I guess he only wanted to get back to

Mom. He ordered my brother and me to go back to bed. We went to sleep after that.

WASTED MONEY

I remember the first time I wasted money. There was a railroad track behind our home in Reading. I had saved up some nickels and dimes for candy, but I was out playing near the railroad tracks with some kids, and I told them to watch what the train did to my nickels and dimes.

I put my coins on the tracks, and we sat there till the train came and ran over them. I got my coins and ran back to my friends to show them how they looked, real cool and flat. We eyeballed them for a few minutes. Then, my friends mentioned to me they were going to the candy store. I looked at my nickels and dimes and knew I was SOL, or shit outta luck.

One more lesson to learn: do not waste money if you want candy.

HAPPY VALLEY

Well, I guess we were in the apartment for about one year when we moved into another section of Reading called Greenfields Manor. The locals called the neighborhood Happy Valley. It was where the army housed the local military men, and it sat behind the Reading airport. They moved the military out, and the poor people moved in.

Down in Happy Valley, there were about twenty barracks with three two-bedroom apartments in each. There were also a few single homes, twenty to twenty-five trailers, two cattle fields, a river, a landing field, and one huge, long hill that came from the main highway. For the kids that lived there, it was a playground you could die for. We didn't know we were poor when we were out playing. In the wintertime, we would go sledding and tobogganing down the hill. In the summertime, we swam in the river. Life was good.

My father finally found a job working as a roofer. My mother also had to work. So, my brother and I had a lot of free time. He was five years younger than me. He had his friends, and I had my own, but, I must say, me and my brother did it all.

We would go into the water drainage pipes under the airport runway. The openings were about five feet in diameter and went down to about ten inches, but to see the tunnel, you would have to crawl about a mile and a half in, which we did. As we were crawling in the pipes, we would pass ladders every few hundred feet up to the top, where the inspection cover plates where. Sometimes, we would climb and lift the plates up and look around. We were right on the runway! We were lucky we didn't get hurt or in trouble.

I remember lying in the cow fields, gazing at the stars and talking about God all night. It was cool. I also remember the cow field had a barbed wire fence with electricity going through it. One day, I, not thinking, began to take a pee near the fence. I turned to talk to a friend and peed right on the wires.

Now, let me tell you, I felt that electric current pass through me.

One more life lesson: do not pee on electric fences.

Also, in the middle of Happy Valley, we had a little store where we would hang out around to watch the girls that shopped. I was just hanging, playing, and living a 1960s life.

I guess it was about 1967 when some toy store had the brilliant idea to store new toys in one of the barracks that had been turned into a warehouse. A few friends and I broke into the warehouse and did some shopping. I guess there were about four or five of us. That was my first B&E. I was fifteen years old. Do you know what toy I took? A bow and arrow set.

After shooting at birds and squirrels for a few days, the cops saw me with my archery set and asked where I acquired it. I remembered not to rat on myself and told them my mother got it for me. They asked me where I lived, put me in the car, and drove me home. Then my mother ratted, admitting to the police she didn't give that bow and arrow set to me. They told my mother about the warehouse break-in and another boy that was involved. My mother made me give the bow and arrow sets to the police. In the end, she had to pay for part of the damage.

My father took the money out on my ass.

INTERESTING PETS

One day, my friend Danny and I climbed up into a tree and chased out a nest of baby squirrels. I caught one and took it home. We named it Matilda and kept it for about a year. That squirrel was so much fun. My father would put peanuts in his pocket, and the squirrel would go in and get them. That was so cool to see. It lived with us until it grew too big for the house. Then, we took it up to my aunt's house. My aunt lived on a ten-acre farm. She would feed the squirrel when it came around.

Other pets we had were the two goats and an ocelot cat from South America. We babysat a young brown bear for the military base in Florida for a few months. I didn't play with the bear too much. It played too rough. A few months passed by with no problems. The animals must have been a nice distraction.

THE FIRECRACKER FRISKY

I believe my life really started after my first burglary. It was the summer of 1968. I met a few boys out the city of Birdsboro, so I started going there a lot. One day, a few of my friends and I were riding around on the outskirts of Birdsboro when we ran across a firecracker company. Way, way out back of the company compound was where they kept the extra-large firecrackers.

We broke into their warehouse and filled eight duffel bags. These firecrackers were about two feet long and one to two feet in diameter. As we were walking back to the getaway car, my friend Danny was trying to cut one open. I didn't see him doing this until he was halfway through it. I said, "Stop being an asshole and put that firecracker back in the bag," and he did.

If that thing went off, he would have been fucked, and some of us might have been fucked, too. My hand to God, it was dumb luck. That means I was very foolish and, at the same time, very lucky.

We got back to the getaway car and put everything in the trunk. Then, we drove back to my friend's home in Birdsboro. His mother and father weren't home, so we pulled the firecrackers out of the trunk. We took them to the back of his house, got them out of the duffel, and pored over them for about a half hour. Then, we wrapped up the booty, and I headed back to Happy Valley. I stashed my firecrackers at a friend's house, then ran home and laid low for a few days.

My friends in Birdsboro lived a few miles away from the much bigger town of Pottstown. Well, back in the late 1960s, the only thing to do at night for fun was ride up and down the main streets of Pottstown.

So here we were—a bunch of kids with large firecrackers cruising up and down Pottstown, where none of us lived. And what do kids do with firecrackers? They light the fuses and throw them, but in the main street of Pottstown, that was not a wonderfully smart thing to do. We blew out the store windows of a whole city block. I was impressed that just one of the jumbo firecrackers could do that. No one was injured. Thank you, God.

It was all over the news and in the papers. There was a massive explosion, and the cops didn't know what happened. A few days went by. I was back at home in Happy Valley. I guess Pottstown is about an hour away from where I lived. I didn't hear a thing about what was happening in Pottstown. So, being the adventurous person that I was, I asked a friend to make me a light steel tube about two feet by two feet so I could carry it with no problem and use it for my firecrackers. He also welded a bottom on and drilled a hole nearby, so I could pull the firecracker fuse out of it and light it.

I still had not heard anything from my crew from Birdsboro about what was going on. So, I kept working on my plan to bring my firecrackers to the top of the cliffs in Mount Penn Preserve and then set them off for all to see. I thought this was a truly cool thing to do. After a few days, my friend gave me a call telling me that my firecracker tube was done. I walked over to pick it up. It was exactly what I was looking for. My friend had also painted it black.

The stage was set. I only had to find a driver. Danny agreed to do it. I said, "This is going to be so cool," and asked him to come pick me up around 10:00 p.m. the next night. We took my car because I had put the tube and four jumbo firecrackers in the trunk. He drove me to the mountain. We got everything out of the trunk and started on a fifteen-minute walk to the top.

Finally, we climbed to the peak. I set the tube up against a humongous boulder and put rocks around the bottom of it to secure it in place. I slid the fattest firecracker down the tube and pulled the fuse out the hole in the bottom. We were set to go. We stashed the other firecrackers around the other side of the boulder. The plan was to light the fuse and run behind another rock, the biggest one there, about fourteen feet away.

We lit the fuse, ran to the safe zone, and dropped down on the ground with our fingers in our ears. Then, all hell broke loose. The first boom took a treetop off and shook the mountain. The second boom set off one of the other firecrackers that we had stashed. I knew that the next boom would surely set the other firecrackers off—and it did. That's when shit really went wild—the mountain shook real hard, rocks started flying everywhere, trees snapped, boom, boom, booms went off all over the place. It was like a warzone. About this time, we started to run. I thought the whole mountain was coming down.

We made it back to the car. We could still hear the firecrackers going off, then fire engines and police cars coming in the distance. We made it back to Happy Valley. Danny headed home, and I went to bed. The next day, it was on the news and in the newspaper.

A few days passed by. I had a visit from the cops and the ATF. The ATF man informed me that they got my name from one of the crew members out of Birdsboro. They told me to give them the firecrackers. They would work on helping me, but only if I handed over the contraband immediately. I knew it was that or go to jail. They were not playing.

We proceeded to my friend's house, and he was home. Danny was about fifteen years older than me, which put him in his late twenties. They asked him about the firecrackers. He said he had taken the firecrackers from me because he didn't want anyone to get hurt, and that he didn't know who to call. He gave the firecrackers back to the police officers, and they took me home. On the way, they must have asked me ten times about the Mount Penn Preserve. I kept saying, "It was not me."

They turned me back over to my mother and took off. I never heard anything from them again. I don't know what happened to the crew out of Birdsboro. I assumed two of the boys got in trouble, but no one else.

FIRST SEX ENCOUNTER

The summer of '68 was an outstanding one. I was learning about girls and about myself. I was turning from a young boy into a young man, but I didn't have anyone to talk to about the changes I was going through. Still, I kept looking.

After a lot of cold showers and late-night trips to the bathroom, and after humping all the trees in the neighborhood, I found that someone. But she was not that special someone that you looked back and had fond memories about. I wish now that I had waited for that special person. Nevertheless, she was the one that brought me to my next step in life. She was not too good-looking, and she had more than a few pounds on her, and I remember that next step in life being very short, a little hurried, but still blissful.

After that day, I was not with her ever again, and I was never the same.

LIFE GOES ON

My boys and I did a lot of Happy Valley fun and games like swimming, fishing, and cardboarding down the big hill. That summer, I not only got laid for the first time, but I also learned about music—the Beatles and the Monkees. I thought life could not get any better.

I was always around older boys. They had cars, and just like in Pottstown, Happy Valley had a main street. Everyone was there trying to get to know girls, and the girls were trying to get to know the boys.

Well, as you know, summers go by pretty fast. It was time to go back to school. That's when I met two meaningful people: my first wife and Zeb, also known as Zapper the Rapper. I gave him that name.

My wife and I lasted little more than a year. I was too young to have a family at sixteen. But I had my first son, Little Dale, whom I love very much. But one thing I learned is that when you're that young and have a kid, you'll never be what you could have been. Your life is not yours anymore, because you live for your kids, not for you.

My friend Zapper the Rapper was with me a lot longer than my wife was. He and I did a lot of out of the norm things over the years. He was an awesome lookout man in a few of my commercial safe burglaries, and for that reason, we also called him Hawk Eye. I will tell you more about him as the story goes on.

After my first wife and I broke up, I moved back in with my mother. My ex-wife and Little Dale kept the trailer. I quit school and kept working to help support my son. My first job was making up electronic circuit boards and drilling tiny holes in them. That job lasted about a year.

CARPENTER STEEL

A few months or so after being home, I started a job at Carpenter Steel, the largest steel plant in Reading. I was only nineteen years old, the youngest man there. I worked as a furnace helper, and I had a good time putting steel ingots into the hot furnace. They would come out the other side and the operator would send them down the mill. Once hot, the metal could be rolled to the size and the length your company would want it—up to one mile long.

That was a cool thing to watch. I worked on that job for a few years.

DOING CREDIT CARD SCAMS

I guess it was about 1972 by now. My friend Danny, or as I started calling him, Dickem' Down Danny, had recently come back from Vietnam, and he turned me on to pot. I liked pot a lot, and I had a lot of fun on pot. It would make me laugh a lot.

1972 was also the year I learned about credit cards and how to scam the card companies. I was partying with this long-haired hippy one day, and he taught me how to get credit cards through the mail, how to use them, and how to get new ones. Each card was worth five hundred. In 1972, that was a lot of money. We would send the credit card applications to the company. About three weeks later, we would have the cards. Now that I had lots of cards, I could go out and meet people who were into things like me.

So I did. I also met a few boys that were in the Pagans, an outlaw motorcycle club. They had weed and speed. I had credit cards. I showed them how to make money. I was around them a lot at first, but they would bring too much heat on themselves, so

I backed off. Under no circumstances did I like that kind of heat on me. I always like to do things my way. I still saw them around. If I needed something, I would call them, and if they needed something, they would call me.

THE TRUCK DEAL

I remember them calling me up and asking me to help them with a truck. They knew I could do this job for them. They had a driver pick me up and take me in the back office of their clubhouse, where I was to have a meeting with their leader. The second in command was there, and he proceeded to tell me what they wanted my help with. He told me that their leader got busted, and the police had taken his twenty-four-foot truck. They needed that rig.

That's when I said, "Quit fucking with me."

To my surprise, he replied, "I'm not fucking with you." He gave me the second set of keys and instructed the driver to show me the semitrailer.

So, we got back into the car and drove to Bern Township Police Station. I knew that building very well. It was four or five miles from Happy Valley. I had walked, played, and driven around the building many times. We passed the building, and he showed me where they were keeping the truck.

"We must do it tonight or tomorrow," the driver said.

I said, "Tomorrow would be good," and asked him to turn around, because we needed to find a place out of the way to switch the load. I lived in the area and knew it well. I guided him back to Happy Valley to show him where we could switch out the goods from the one truck and into the other. It was a large pasture where I had played when I was young. After I showed him, he took me home.

The next afternoon, we touched base with each other. I met with him and told him I would need someone to drop me off about one mile from the police headquarters. I purchased a pair of walkie-talkies with three different frequency channels with my credit cards. The stage was set.

I called him up and said, "I will need a ride around midnight," and the driver was right on schedule. Then, he dropped me off at the designated spot. I walked around for an hour and a half, keeping my eyes on the police building the whole time. The place was quiet.

I made my move. I walked over to the cab, opened the door, put the key in the engine, and turned it on. I pulled out of the parking area nice and easy. About halfway to the pasture, I called and raised them on the walkie-talkie. I said, "I got the prize."

I pulled into the field, backed it up to the back of the waiting vehicle, and got out. The motorcycle boys were notably happy to see the truck. There were about six men there. The boss told my original driver to get me the hell out of there, and that's what he did.

I went home to sleep and woke up around noon. I read the day's newspaper, and on the front page: *Truck Stolen from Police Compound by Motorcycle Gang*.

The boys called me up to meet with them after about a week or so. I cruised over to their clubhouse. When I walked into that place, it was full of women, bikers and me. It certainly was one hell of a night.

CREDIT CARDS ENDING

Well, me and the boys from Happy Valley had an excellent time for the next few months. The credit card scams were coming to an end because for new cards, you needed a good address to mail them to. The good news was there were a lot of people that would let you use their address for illegal mail. My friend and I used each other's addresses for new cards, and our cards arrived after four weeks. We were having a high time, when one day, a postal inspector came to my mother and father's home, asking about the person who was supposed to have lived at this address. Not once did I tell my mother or father about this, so no one knew anything.

The postal inspector said, "This address was used for getting illegal credit cards." We all informed him we didn't know anything. He said, "Okay," and, hard to believe, he went on his way. We didn't have anything more to do with the cards.

Dumb luck again: I was dumb and very lucky. I was never into taking money from the working man, only large businesses. I used no guns—just brains to get their money.

LOVE AND MEXICO

Everything went back to normal for a while. I met a girl named Linda. Her father owned three or four bakeshops in and around

Reading. She landed me a job working with her father, and he taught me how to bake cakes, cupcakes, cookies—all the goodies we all love to eat.

I loved to bake. It was close to a year when I asked him for a week's vacation. He said, "Go and have a good time."

So I announced to Linda, "We are going to do something cool." We were going down to Texas to see Zapper the Rapper. He lived only a few hours from Mexico.

Linda and I drove to Austin to party with Zeb. I must tell you, I love Texas very much. We partied for a few days, and then, with me driving Linda's new BMW, Zeb took us to Laredo, Texas. It's a border town on the Rio Grande. We headed south at about 3:00 p.m. for shopping and dinner. It was over ninety degrees out. We were dining, and we started to drink and smoke some weed.

So, we were feeling good, and Zeb started to tell us about Nuevo Laredo, Mexico, just across the river. All the shops were real cheap, and outside town was something called "Boys' Town" which he said was a whore town with fifteen-foot walls around it. There was one way in and one way out, and he wanted to go there. I was surprised that Linda wanted to see this as well.

We hailed a cab and headed in. As you passed in through the main gate, the police station was on your right. The police didn't stop you going into Boy's Town, but they might stop you coming out.

The cab dropped us off, and we started to walk around, stepping into the packed clubs. There were three roads going one way and three roads going the other way. Other sights to see in Boys' Town were their seven massive nightclubs. They also had about ten small-scale clubs. When you walked in a club, the young, beautiful Mexican women would run up to you and ask in their broken English, "You want to fucky sucky?" Back then, it was $5 for a blowjob and $10 or $15 to get laid.

My favorite was this medium-sized club, though. You walked into this club, and there were tables on both sides of you, with the bar straight ahead. To one side was a door that led to pools—actual pools with water in them—and a bridge that you could cross into a room with a jukebox. This became my favorite club in Boy's Town. It still is to this day. Tomikas is the name of this club if you ever get there and you're wondering. But I will tell you more about this, and the back room, in another story.

When you came out of the Tomikas club doors and went to the left, the next club, my friends, is where the donkey show is—where the donkey does the girl. Now you know a little about Mexico and where I go.

We danced, drank, and smoked, and Zeb went with a few of the girls. I guess it was now about 2:00 a.m. We got into a cab back at the gate, and that's when a guard asked us to get out of the vehicle. They wanted to see Linda's papers. I guess it was easier to come in when you're a girl than to get out. They thought she was a working girl. We had to go into the station and talk to the head cop there. After a few hours of fighting, he let us go.

We crawled into another cab, and he took us back into Boy's Town. We were still drunk as hell walking around town. I found this Mexican dude selling switchblade knives and bought about ten of them. At that time, we decided to go back to the hotel room in Laredo. Now I had knives that I had to hide to get them into Texas. Being as drunk as I was, I pulled the ashtray out of its holder and threw the knives in behind that. I then put the ashtray back into its holder.

I started the car and drove to the bridge. On the US side, they stopped us and asked if we were US citizens. We gave them our paperwork. Then, they asked us to get out of the car. They checked over the car about five times. I thought I was going to jail, but that didn't happen. They looked and looked and looked, but found nothing. They had to let us go. We headed back to the room.

The next day, we went on our way back to Austin. We dropped Zapper the Rapper back at his home and headed back to Happy Valley.

Linda and I only went out together for a few more months after we came back from Texas. I moved on.

LEARNING TO DANCE

I was twenty-one, working more at Carpenter Steel, no longer at the bakery, earning enough money to go out to bars. I was trying to learn how to dance. I went out all over town every Friday and Saturday and tried to disco and rock & roll. After about fifty women wanted to throw up on me from motion sickness, I started to get my groove and became smooth, graceful. I also permed my hair. I went from flat to fluffy. I bought a pair of platform shoes and hit all the hot discos in town. I started to get to know a lot of women and a lot of the men who knew how to get around that town.

MEETING BIG G

One night while I was out, I ran into a guy named Big G. I didn't know how this one person would change my life. I went to a club that was a hotspot in Reading, and after a few drinks, I shuffled out on the dance floor and saw Big G having fun with two beautiful women. I shimmied up, cut in, and started to dance with the one I liked. They asked me if I wanted to sit with them, and I did. We had one hell of a good time. We swapped phone numbers and made plans to meet again.

Big G and the two women left before me, and when they were gone, I asked an acquaintance, "Who was that guy?"

He filled me in. Big G was a master thief with the Diamond Gang out of Reading. I was an adventurous person who liked anything out of the norm, even outside the law, and I was intrigued. A few weeks passed by, then one day, Big G gave me a call and asked if we could meet.

I told him we could meet at the Chef's Lounge bar in Reading on Ninth Street, Friday around 8:00 p.m. and added, "If that's okay with you."

He said, "That's fine." I know he had found out who I was, and he knew that I had found out about him.

Friday night came. We met and had a great time. We became fast friends, and we are still friends to this day.

After we knew each other for a few months, he asked me to move a few things for him. I took the stuff he gave me and sold them. We were making good money. I was meeting a lot of the big boys in Reading, the real people that ran the city.

Before long, I was selling thousands of cigarettes and pills to the main people in town. Life was fantastic.

Even at Carpenter Steel, I was learning a lot and moving forward quickly. I moved from furnace helper to overhead crane operator. They taught me how to move very large things. It was a pretty cool job. Everything was going well for me. I had a lot of money and was living the good life. Things could not have been better.

THE FIRST RAT

Then it happened. I was living in Mount Penn in a three-bedroom house. I had a compartment in my bathroom wall made specifically for stashing things. It was mostly for drugs and money; this particular part of the wall cost me about a thousand to have done. You could not tell it was there.

I remember the day. I was going out of my house. This guy I had recently met was coming to see me. He knew a friend of mine. He asked me if I had this one type of pill. I said, "Yes. I have some other pills for sale, too." He then wanted to know the price for all of them. I told him it would cost him about $18,000 for all the pills he was asking about.

We were inside my home at this time. He wanted to take about five hundred dollars' worth as samples to show his people. I instructed him to stay downstairs. I proceeded to go upstairs and returned with the pills, and I gave them to him. He gave me the money and asked how long it would take me to get the rest of the pills if he came up with the eighteen thou.

"Not long. Just give me a call," I said, and he left.

What happened next was crazy. I remember going out of my home and, on my way to the car, my stomach got out of control. I felt like shit for some reason. I got into my car and drove to the stop sign, and that's when all hell broke loose.

Undercover cops came out of the woodwork. The next thing I knew, I was handcuffed and lying on the ground. Then, they announced they had a warrant to search my house, and they had an arrest warrant, too. They pulled me off the ground, and we walked back to my house half a block away. When we approached the door, I gave them the key. We walked in. They put me on the couch and told me to stay there. So I did.

I guess about eight to ten undercover police officers were going through my entire house. They kept asking me where I got my drugs. I stated, "I need to speak to my attorney."

I sat there for two hours, and they had nothing. They were still busting my balls about where the drugs were and who my people were. I kept stating the same thing. I needed to speak to my attorney.

Now, we were going into four and a half hours. I told them I had to pee, maybe take a dump. They wanted me to hold it. I said, "I'll try." I was trying to get into the bathroom, where the drugs were, and at the same time trying to keep them out. I guess it was five hours now when I told them I had to go to the bathroom again.

The main undercover guy yells, "Send him up!" meaning to the bathroom, where he was. They allowed me to get up, walked me over to the stairs, and told me to go up. The leading officer was waiting for me at the top of the stairs and walked me into the bathroom. He took off the handcuffs, and as I walked into the bathroom past where the drugs were, I gave the stash spot a hard look.

That was my mistake. He was watching me like a hawk. I tried to look away quick, but it wasn't fast enough. I took my pee, and he sent me down back on the couch.

At this time, I started to pray, but I guess I was too late. All I heard was banging and more banging. After ten or fifteen minutes, I knew they had found my stash, and it was not a little stash, either. I had over $25,000 worth of pills, plus bottles of morphine, Demerol, etc. (Adjusting for inflation, today that would be more worth than $128,000.) After about one more hour, they brought the paddy wagon over to pick me up, took me to City Hall, and locked me up.

The next day, I had a bail hearing, and they set my bail at $50,000.

I got in touch with my people and told them not to worry about my bail, but to get a solid attorney, and I would go in for a bail reduction when the time was right. The newspapers had a picture of my home on the front page. It read: *L. Dale Johnson busted with the biggest haul of pills in Reading history: $26,000 in all kinds of pills found behind a false panel in the wall in the second-floor bathroom.*

THE SETUP

I was plain dumb at twenty-one years of age. But I liked the excitement of wheeling and dealing. There I was, sitting in Berks County Prison, and I knew a few of the inmates. One inmate told me to meet him in the TV room, or dayroom, as some people called it. When we met, he said he had some weed for me. He gave me a half ounce, and I put it in my pocket. After a few minutes passed, we were just bullshitting, and he was called out of the room by a guard.

At this time, the hardcore guards came into the day room and said to us fifteen or so inmates, "It's time for a shakedown."

You can imagine what happened next. The guards grabbed me, ordered me to put my hands on the wall, and started to pat me down. They found the weed. They asked me how I got a hold of this much weed in the jail.

I stated, "I need to speak to my attorney." I knew at that time I'd been set up for this fall. But to this day, I do not know who set me up or why.

They took me to the hole, under the jail. At that time, I was honestly the most disliked man in the Reading jail. The next day, the one inmate that cleaned up the cells slid me a newspaper. Again, there I was in print, this time with the biggest bust in Berks County Prison history: *The inmate that got busted was L. D. Johnson, the same one that got busted with the most drugs in Reading history.*

After being set up at the jail, I was marched to another bail hearing, now for the weed bust. It was set at $15,000–$20,000. I wasn't feeling too good about myself at this time in my life.

STARTING A NEW BUSINESS

Well, after a few weeks, Big G got me out on bail. I took off to meet with my crew and announced that I would need to fix this thing as much as possible. They told me the situation would work out just fine for me. They had talked to some people already.

I knew I would need a lot of money. I liked my job at the steel mill, but that would not give me the amount I needed. Still, I went back to work there, because I knew that the police were watching me undoubtedly very closely and this would keep the heat off me a little bit. So, I started running an overhead crane again. But after a few weeks, I knew this job was not going to take me where I needed to be.

I called Big G up and stated plainly, "I need to make money."

He said, "We'll have to go out and get some."

Here I was out on bail and starting a new business: safe burglary. I do not know what it was with me. I cannot stand to be like other people, but don't ask me why, because I don't know. I just like living on the edge.

I do want to let you know that I was a commercial burglar. We did banks, supermarkets, drugstores, clubs like American Legion, Veterans of Foreign Wars, etc. They were all done with finesse—no guns.

Back to the story, I was out on bail, getting ready to do safe burglaries. I met with Big G, Bill, and Little Joe; they called themselves the Diamond Gang. Big G took me to his apartment. He started to show me how to work with walkie-talkies and scanners, so we could listen to the police and what they were doing. I thought this was the coolest thing ever.

I started as a driver and a lookout man. When we went out, we would have two cars—one for the drop off and pick up, and the other as an emergency getaway car. That one, we'd park far from the score, or the place we were going to do the job. The cars were old police cars we had bought from an auction.

We'd bring an "in-tool bag" to get into the score. It had screwdrivers, large and small, a hammer, punches, a crowbar, walkie-talkies, and a portable scanner. The "torch bag" had an acetylene torch set with a portable oxygen bottle and an acetylene bottle. They showed me how to work all the equipment and cars, and it was time to go out. There were three or four of us that would go out and make money.

My first job was an outside lookout at a VFW post up around the Allentown/Easton area. We drove up the week before the job and took a few hours to walk around and watch the score around the same time of day as when we would do the actual job. We would also find quiet places to park. If it met our criteria, we would come up the next week.

On the night of, we would park the emergency car first. Then, we would pick up that driver in the car we were going to use for the score. We would then drive around the score and see if things still scoped out. If it satisfied us, I would then drive to a dark area and get the tools out of the trunk. I'd then drive to the drop-off area and let my crew out. If everything was lovely, I would wait at the designated parking area.

Everything was going well, so I stepped out of the car walked to the lookout area. I could see everything, the VFW and all the roads. I had the hand scanner with me, so I could hear all the police calls. If they received a call for the address where the club was, I would hear it. I also had a walkie-talkie with me. The other men had a walkie-talkie with them.

I gave the guys the "green light" that they could go to work.

They crept to the side door and took about thirty seconds to get in.

They called for a green light. I said, "Everything is green."

They told me to stay on my toes and checked with me a few times, asking me for more green lights. After doing that for just twenty minutes, they asked me again for a green light and a pickup. I said, "Everything is green, and the pickup will be in a few minutes."

I was a new man at this type of work and thought something was wrong. How could they crack a safe and clean out the place that quickly? I drove to the pickup area, and they were there. I popped the trunk, they put everything in the trunk, they got in, and I drove off. After a few minutes of silence, they said, "Everything went good."

They told me to head over to the other car. We put the money into the other vehicle. We would keep the money and the tools apart from each other, just in case one of the cars was stopped. For the same reason, the cars would go two different ways. Then, we would all meet back at the garage, or stash house, as we called it. We pulled the car with the tools into the stash house and parked the car with the money on the street.

We took the money out of the car, took it into the stash house, and counted it. It came to about $6,000. There were three of us. We had made $2,000 each for a few hours of being in the hot zone. The hot zone was the time you spent in any place where you could go to jail if you were caught.

We split up the money. I wanted to know everything about the score. I needed to know how they worked so fast. They explained to me that the safe was on day lock, which meant you would turn the dial to the right and it would go to the last number of the combination and open. A few scores were like that. Fast. Easy. We then cleaned all the tools up and made sure everything was ready for the next score.

There were a few clubs and a drugstore I did within a few months. I liked doing drugstores. We would take the drugs and all the cigarettes and do some shopping while we were there. We would each fill up a few trash bags of everything we could, even regular household items. In all honesty, I loved that kind of nightlife. Being out there with professional thieves was exciting.

JAIL TIME

Now, it was time to go to the Reading courthouse for sentencing for the drug charges. They offered me a deal: nine months to five years. Of course, I took the deal. They also gave me two weeks to get my affairs together and then report to Berks County Prison. Two weeks passes fast when jail is waiting.

I reported in as scheduled. They gave me a prison suit and other prison clothes. Then, they put me in solitary. Everyone spends one week in quarantine. After that, the main population.

Everyone had to work in jail, and everyone liked cakes and cookies, guards and inmates alike. So, after quarantine, thanks to my ex, Linda, and her dad, the bakeshop owner in Reading, I put my baking skills to work and started a job in the kitchen. I knew a lot of people in BCP, so when I returned to the main population, it felt like Old Home Week (a town reunion festival that was common to this part of Pennsylvania when I was young). Everyone came up to say hello and tell me how lucky I was with the sentence I received. Funny, I didn't feel very lucky.

I was there for a few weeks and the next thing I knew, I was on my way to the big house. Keep in mind, I was only twenty-one at the time. The state bus came and picked me up to take me to the State Pen in Bellefonte. It was a three- to four-hour ride to the state correctional institution, and Rockview Penitentiary was huge. When you arrived there, you had to spend time in a separate area from the other inmates again, until they processed you into the main population. I was what they called a short timer. They put me in the east wing with a kitchen job.

Things were going as best they could in jail. I would work out all the time and run a lot. Time was going fast for me. After about three months, I found a job outside on the farm. I remembered it was hay season. I would go out and walk behind a wagon, throwing up hay bales all day long. I didn't care for that job much, so I took a job in the sawmill. I liked cutting trees into boards. A few months flew by, and I only had three and a half more to go.

My counselor informed me that a new program was coming in—learning how to drive a tractor-trailer. I said, "I'd like to learn how to drive a big truck." I called my crew on the outside and told them what I was doing. They wished me good luck. We didn't talk about it again.

I started truck driving school. It was a six-week course. We had two weeks of learning about the truck—how to hook up and unhook the trailer, how to hook up and unhook the airlines, how to check the whole trailer and truck, etc. Now, it was time to go out on the road and drive.

We drove within a fifty-mile radius of the jail. We were all over that area, and I liked that very much. I was away from jail. It was hard to go back after being out on the road all day but being on the road made those six weeks of jail time go fast. I completed the course and earned my certificate.

I took a job cutting grass and had my people on the outside bring me some weed and vodka. It was time to party, and I did. For a few weeks, I didn't tell anyone that I had these things, because people would rat you out. Then it was time to go in front of the parole board.

I met with them, and they granted me parole, but the catch was I'd have to wait about six weeks for my parole papers, and they would give me my date of parole then.

After eight long weeks, I was released.

• • • • • • • • • • • • •

PART II

STARTING OVER

I remember the bus ride clearly. Early 1976. I was wondering the whole trip home what I was going to do about a job. I didn't have a high school diploma, and I had a drug bust on my record. After the four-hour ride, we pulled into the Reading Bus Terminal. No one was there to meet me. I felt all alone at this time in my life.

I made it to my mother's new, two-bedroom apartment. I took the second room. It had no bed, but a rug. I showed up around 5:00 p.m. She fed me and gave me a good talking to. She told me I would have to get a job as soon as I could, and that I must stay out of trouble. If I had a normal life, she said, I could stay there as long as I wanted. I said, "Thank you, Mom. Love you."

Then, I went to my room to contemplate what I was going to do with my life. While lying on the rug on the floor, thinking which way I was going to go, it hit me. I would make what would be one of the biggest decisions in my life. I didn't want to live a normal life.

After fighting with myself for a few days, I made my decision final. I didn't want to spend my life working for a car payment, a house payment, and keeping my five other partners happy—the phone company, gas company, car company, oil company, and the electric company. So, the next day, I made a phone call. I called Big G, and he told me where to meet him.

We met at a bar. I walked in, and he was already there, waiting. He said, "Hello, Kid." I was the youngest man in the crew, and they all called me Kid.

I said, "How are you?"

He said he was okay.

"Me too, but I would like to have some money and a woman," I said. He assured me he would work on those things. We talked for a few more minutes, and then he asked me what I was going to do. "I'm going to make money," I said, and he laughed.

He made it known that we would be on the road tomorrow, and he would pick me up around 10:00 a.m. After a few more drinks, we got into his car, and he took me home. I packed for the road trip and hit the hay.

By 10:00 a.m., I was in one of Big G's old cop cars. He mentioned that he had the tools with him and was hoping we were going to make some money that night. He had a few places up in Northern Pennsylvania on his list, and we were going to survey them first.

After two days, we narrowed our list down to five spots that showed promise, but there was this one club we liked a lot for parking, for money, and for a quick in. It was the Fraternal Order of Eagles Club. We called the other crew member we wanted on this job and told him to grab the other tools from the stash house and come up the next day. We headed off to find a room.

Talking about getting a room, sometimes it took a few tries to land shelter, because everything we filled out on each motel register was a lie, and we needed a place that wasn't going to check our credentials. We always stayed forty-five minutes or so from the score. We would do that because the police would only check local motels.

Back to the story, Little Joe arrived. We explained the plan to him in detail and told him to relax a bit, that we could go look-see the score in an hour or so. This was the first time I had seen Little Joe since I had gotten out of jail. He fucked with me a little and asked me if I had a girlfriend in jail. I said, "I don't play like that."

Time passed, and we all walked to the car. I drove us to the score and showed Little Joe. He liked it. We drove him around, so he could get the full feeling of the score. After he saw all he needed to, we drove back to the room to rest. One of us ducked out for food and drinks while the other two stayed in the room. That's how it always worked. We didn't want to be seen together outside the room.

The next day, it was time to go to work. Little Joe checked the tools out in Reading before he left town. We took the tools out of Little Joe's car and put them in the old police car. We then took Little Joe's car and parked it five miles from the score. I pulled in and picked up Little Joe. I drove past the score, and everything was mellow. I then drove to the drop-off area, and they jumped out. I popped the trunk. They grabbed the tools.

Big G handed me a walkie-talkie, and off they went. Because I was on parole, I had to be the outside lookout. I drove to the parking area and waited. I got out and made my way over to the lookout area. Everyone got into position. They asked for a green light. I reported to them they had a green light. They slipped in. We didn't talk unless we had to. About one hour later, they asked for a green light. I said again, "Everything is green."

They told me to get the car, and so I did and picked them up. I popped the trunk. They put the tools and the money in the trunk and hopped in with me. I drove them to the other car. They told me to pop the trunk to separate the money from the tools. They took the money in Little Joe's car. They directed me to meet them back at the room and to park that car on the street next to the motel. I said, "Okay."

After driving an hour, I parked the car where they had said. I got to the room and knocked on the door. They opened it, and there was money all over my bed. We had hit a club that had punch-board gambling. A lot of them back in the day had that illegal type of gaming.

They briefed me that the safe was a puncher. That meant that you knock the dial off the safe and then hit the pin that the dial was on with a hammer and a punch. As you hit the pin, you wiggle the handle until the safe opens.

For being in the hot zone for about an hour and a half, we made just over $4,000 each—more than a $12,000 score. We put our bags and money in the clean car. Little Joe and Big G drove that, while I drove the hot vehicle back to the stash house. I arrived there discreetly, put the car in the stash house, walked around to where we were going to meet, and they were there. I got into the car. They took me to my mother's, and we said our goodbyes.

I walked into my mother's house and motioned to say hello, and she asked me if I went out and got laid. I acknowledged, "Yes," and turned to my room. Here I was, fresh out of jail for four days, and I had broken about ten laws that would put me back in for a long time, and I hadn't even gotten laid yet.

The next day, I went out to buy clothes and a car. Then I thought, *Why don't I get laid?* After nine months without making love, not even feeling a woman's touch, it was time. I ran around where I knew a few women, and I saw one I knew. I picked her up, and we cruised to a motel and had a good time.

After that, I set out to locate an apartment. I found one on Tenth Street. It was a one-bedroom, and the inside was nice. I went out and picked up everything I needed for it. Within a week or so, my life was back to the norm. I took a job as a shipping and receiving clerk. I always kept a job to keep the heat off me. I also put the word out on the street that I was on the lookout for the rat that gave me up—the one that came to my house for the pill samples.

THE BUTTER DEAL

A few weeks had passed by when I got a call from my crew. They updated me about "the butter deal." I recall they wanted to put what I had learned at the Rockview truck driving school to the test. They showed me where they kept a truck full of butter at a factory. The mob in Ohio wanted the butter, so we drove out to Kutztown, dairy country, and checked out the job, and I said, "I'm in."

We had to wait for Sunday. A few more days passed, and it was time.

We met. There were five of us doing this score. We took the main car out of the garage with some tools and drove to the butter warehouse. It was 3:00 a.m. when we arrived. We picked out two trucks, hotwired them, and off we went. We made it to the warehouse near Allentown. We backed one truck up to the dock and started to unload the butter into the warehouse. We unloaded one truck, moved it out of the way, then backed up the other truck to the dock and started to unload that one.

Now, I guess, it was around noon on Sunday when a police car came pulling up to the warehouse. I ran up to the top of the warehouse, looking for a way out. But, to my surprise, he only wanted to know why we were working on Sunday. One of the crew members informed him we had a special order we had to get out.

He bought it and left.

We finished unloading the trucks. We then closed the warehouse and drove the hot trucks to Philadelphia. We did that to put the heat on the Philadelphia boys. After that, we flew back to the warehouse to load the butter into a clean truck. We loaded the truck, then we all headed home to take a break. The driver that was taking the truck to Ohio was to be there at 6:00 a.m. Monday morning.

He overslept, and, wouldn't you know it, that cop came back because the barracks got a call about two trucks missing in Kutztown. He put two and two together. They came back to check out what he'd seen Sunday, and he busted the main boy in Allentown for the butter heist. Truthfully, I was a little nervous about this information when I heard it. I'd only been out of jail for a few months, and this was one of the big boys out of Allentown. He didn't tell anyone about the other men. God bless you, Pete.

Circumstances had it, if our driver had been on time, the people in Ohio would have had cheap butter, and my crew and I would have had money. Oh well—on to the next exciting thing.

THE RAT'S EX-WIFE

I got news on the rat. His ex-wife was hanging out with this someone I knew. So, I mentioned to this someone that I would like to meet her. They told me it would take about a week or so. I said we should all go out to a good dinner, and they said, "Okay."

About a week went by, and it was time to meet the ex-wife of the rat. I was never the one to hurt anyone, but I would get even ten times over. I drove to the meeting place.

My friend brought the ex-wife in. What I saw was a beautiful woman. I had money, so we went out for a real nice dinner. Then, we went out to a few bars, and it was all my treat. The whiskey was flowing, and we all had one hell of a wonderful time. At the end of the night, she went her way, and I went my way.

We would meet again soon, and we agreed: we didn't like losers. We had different reasons.

SEEING AND IDENTIFYING A BODY

I kept working at the shipping and receiving warehouse to keep the heat off me. I guess a month had blown by when my supervisor confided in me that he went to the doctor, and the doctor said he should go to the hospital. He needed work done on his heart. He confessed to me he was not going. I told him to go. For whatever reason, he didn't. A few more days went by, and he let me know he was going out for lunch.

I told him, "Go for it."

The next thing I knew, I was called into the office. The main boss informed me that my supervisor was dead in his car about three blocks away, and he wanted me to identify the body. I went with hesitation.

I drove to the scene, got out of my car, and met the cops. They asked me if I was there to identify the body. I responded with a yes. We walked over to the car, and I looked in. What a sight that was. I told the cop it was him. That was a hard thing to do. That guy was cool, and I saw that picture in my mind for a while.

After a few days, the big boss called me into his office. *Here I go again*, I thought. This time, he asked if I could run the shipping warehouse.

I said, "I can, but need more money."

He said, "Okay," so I returned to work.

I was never in on Mondays because I was out looking for a score to do. The boss never said anything to me, because everything was going great. I was making everyone work hard, and I was shipping more parts out than this company ever had. So, when I took off on Mondays, the boss would not get pissed off. Little did I realize, by pushing my men over four days, we were setting records. So, when I got a letter from the main office praising me for my accomplishments, I went in for a pay raise. When I told my supervisor what I wanted, he almost shit himself. He needed some time to think about it.

THE DRUGSTORE B&E

The next thing we did was a drugstore up around the eastern part of Pennsylvania. We did our usual drill. I found my way to the safe, a small, inconspicuous square-door that we opened in about thirty minutes. Then, we snagged the drugs, took the smokes, and did a little "shopping" on our way out. We had a van on this score. We had about one thousand cartons of cigarettes. It was up to me to move everything.

We had all the uppers and downers you could dream of. We had morphine, Demerol, and a bottle of 99.9 percent cocaine flakes from the Merck pharmaceutical company. We loved these and called them "Merck Flakes." The boys didn't know shit about drugs, and that was cool. I gave them what they wanted for the Merck flakes to use with the girls.

I always made out with those boys. I sold the cigarettes for six dollars a carton, giving us six grand for the cigarettes. We stole about six grand out of the safe, as well. I sold the drugs for about nine grand. For two and a half hours in the hot zone, we pulled $21,000 and split that up three ways. That money would last me a long time.

FINDING THE PERFECT SCORE

I kept going out looking for scores. I must tell you, it was hard work. You have to drive all over the states where you work, look, and look some more until you find that perfect score. And we worked in a lot of states. We would keep a list of the scores we saw and then rate them. The "A" scores were the ones we would do right away—the best ones. A "B" score looked good but had some issues. A "C" score was so-so, probably wouldn't bring much money or would take too long. A "D" score was, of course, a dog. But we still put D scores on the list if we had nothing else to do and we needed the money. But of course, we always tried to do the A scores.

LITTLE JOE TAKES A BUST

I remember a score up in Milesburg. After being on the road for a few days looking, we spotted a perfect score we all liked. It was a club, an American Legion. Big G, Little Joe, and I traveled up to do this score. The funny part of this story is that Rockview Penitentiary was less than seven miles away.

We drove up there after we took the tools out of the other car. I dropped them off and parked. We all met around the back of the score and got in through the back door. They started to work on the safe using the punch method. Somehow, someone heard them and called the cops.

I saw the cars pull up with no siren or lights on, but I knew it was a bust. I yelled to the boys, "It's a rumble! Get out fast!"

We ran to the back door and opened it. Standing about ten feet away was a cop! So, we ran to the side door. It looked clear. Little Joe ran out and tried to jump over the four-foot fence, but he got hung up on it. The cop caught him.

Big G and I turned back, ran out the back door, and got away. We hustled back to the car and drove the hell out of town. I dropped off Big G at the other vehicle, and we didn't stop driving until we hit Reading.

ATTORNEY FEES

When one of our crew got busted, we helped pay for their attorney, and if they went to jail, we sent them money.

I was back to work on Tuesday, as usual, and we laid low for a few weeks until we got Little Joe out on bail. We always used Johnny Banana as our bail bondsman. Once Little Joe was out, of course, we needed to make money. So, we hit the road the next weekend. The rule with my crew was: if you're out on bail or parole, you cannot go inside; you must be a driver and outside lookout. We set out, did a few clubs, and made some money. Little Joe worked with my crew and ran his own crew. He was doing his thing. Big G and I were doing our thing!

BIG G TAKES A BUST

Months later, after things had died down and we were getting low on funds, I brought up a C score to Big G. It had been on my mind for a while: a good supermarket we'd found in Clymer a few months back. He also remembered it. So, Big G and I drove up and put it on the list. I liked that market a lot, and so did Big G.

We went up with this guy, Duke, and looked at it again. Duke ran with Big G before I came into the picture. We decided to do it that weekend.

The night came to do the score. I dropped them off with the tools and parked the car. We met up at the lookout area, moved to the back door, and got in. We had the scanner going and made our way to the safe. It was a heavy, two-door safe—one square door on the top and one on the bottom. I moseyed to the lookout area while Duke and Big G worked on the top safe. They punched the top one in thirty minutes. It came open, and there were stacks of cash in it—over ten grand, we guessed.

I had a mop bucket there for the money. We always put our money in a mop bucket, because it had wheels on the bottom and was easy to move around. I rolled it over, and then we got busy on the bottom safe. We knocked the dial off and tried to punch the pin through, and wouldn't you know it—we hit a tear gas canister. We tried putting water on it, hoping it would help, but it didn't work.

Thinking back, we could have taken the thousands in cash that we had and gotten out of danger. But, being who we were, we sat back and tried to figure out where the nearest fire company was because we knew they had gas masks. This was not the first time we had hit tear gas in a safe. Big G and I secured our tools and money out back and took off. Duke stayed in the market, so he could let us back in.

We knew there was a fire station about four blocks away. As we were walking up the back alley, the dogs started to go off. It was wintertime, and you would think the dog owners would let their pets in the house. But they did not. A lot of dogs started barking, which was bad for us. We made it to the fire company, and no one was around.

We snuck in the side door. We found the gas masks and headed back to the score. We decided to walk down the street, not the alley where the dogs were. We had nearly made it back to the supermarket when we spotted a cop, so we ducked behind a shed.

The cop must have seen us and yelled, "Stop. Come out!"

We started to run up the alley, and he followed us. We turned up an alley between two row homes. The cop was on our ass. As we came out of the alley, Big G escaped right, down the next alley and between some houses. I fled left.

The cop followed Big G. Somehow, we wound up crossing paths a block down and hid behind two sheds. The cop was close. We could hear him right in front of the shed. I backed out the other way, and Big G ran right into the cop while holding the stolen gas mask. This guy tackled Big G, cuffed him, and put him in the car.

While all that was going on, I rolled out the mop bucket with the money. Duke was there and picked up the tools. We made it back to the car and put the money and tools in the trunk. I got behind the wheel, and off we went. I could see four cop cars searching around the supermarket as I sped away.

We made it back to Reading, then ditched the car and tools in the stash house. We took the money to my apartment, and when we were done counting it, we had each made $4,000. Surprisingly, there was $12,000 in that safe. It made me wonder how much was in the other one. Duke asked me to keep Big G's money and bail him out with it, so I stashed his cut with mine back at the house.

I went to work the next day. I was on standby until Johnny Banana got Big G out on bail. Six days had gone by when I got a call from Big G to meet him at his house after work. I gave him his money and my part of his bail, and then I gave him a thousand, so he would have a little money to put down for an attorney. We sat and talked for a little while, and then I headed home.

GETTING THE EVIDENCE

The next day, he called me and asked what the cops would do with the evidence. I knew they would keep it in the evidence room in the police station. He told me, "We have to get the evidence out of the police station."

I stared at the phone like he was nuts.

He went on, "Look, this is a small town, and we know the cops go home around three or four in the morning. Are you in or out?"

I could only say, "Look, Big G, you're asking me to go and break into a police station, and you want me to tell you yes or no right now? I'll have to think about this."

He needed me to let him know before the weekend. I must say, this was a serious thing he wanted me to help him with. Friday came, and he called me to meet up. I went to the meet and spat it out: "I'm in."

We took off, fetched the work car and some light tools, and drove to Clymer, Pennsylvania. We always got a room thirty to forty miles away from the score. On the way, we talked about how we were going to do the score on the police headquarters. I guess it was about 11:00 p.m. when we got settled. We agreed to go up there Saturday morning to study the place, to find parking and an innocent place to watch. We would watch the place from 12:00 a.m. to 4:00 or 5:00 a.m.

We woke up around 10:00 a.m. and decided to bring the tools into the room and set up the hand scanner with the police frequency for that town. We wanted to be plugged into them and see what was going locally, if anything. We put the tools in the closet. When we paid for the room, we told them they did not have to clean the room (or get a look at our kits.)

We knew where we were going. We grabbed a quick sandwich. We couldn't risk being recognized, so we moved at a fast pace. We got into town. Nothing was going on with the scanner. Clymer was a small town of about fifteen hundred. We made our way to the northwest area. We came upon the supermarket where Big G got busted. We continued for four or five blocks, and the police headquarters was on our left side. Then, we went about five or six more blocks. We drove by the headquarters at a medium pace. We didn't want anyone to see us. Things were peachy. We saw nothing of concern around the building at all.

Now, we looked for parking. It took us about one hour to find a secure location for the car. We saw everything we needed to see. We headed back to the motel. Let me tell you, this was the first police headquarters I had ever burglarized. It would be my last, too. I guess Big G was stewing about tonight because he was not talking much.

A few thoughts were going through my little brain. One of them was, *I wish I would have told one of my crew members to bring another car, just in case I needed another way out of town.* Then I thought, *Who would want to be involved in this type of situation?* I knew no one.

We stopped for a six-pack of beer as we were making our way back to the motel. We got inside our room, and I got the weed out. We smoked a joint and had a beer. We relaxed for about five hours. Then we got the tools out of the closet, and we wiped them down—we didn't want any prints. No mistakes. We had to be on our toes. We reviewed the plan a few times.

"We are going to be in a little wooded area across the street from the headquarters, and our car will be about four blocks from the score," I explained. "We could do just a look-over tonight. I know where everything is, I don't need a look-over. But, if you do, we will go and do one and then do the score on Sunday. None of the bars are open at that time in the morning. It'll be dead around town."

Big G sat back and thought for a few minutes. He was okay with doing the score on Sunday—less risky—but he wanted the look-over. I was cool with that. We set the alarm for 11:00 p.m., and the time sure did go fast.

We walked to the car. We were set to do nothing but a little recon on the score tonight and only needed to take a scanner and two flashlights. We headed for the score, nonstop. We arrived at about 12:30 a.m.

We drove by the place, and no one was there. It was dead on the scanner—nothing but bullshit calls. We continued for another mile and found a satisfactory place to unload the tools. I pulled over and popped the trunk. Big G jumped out and got the bag out. He and the tools were in the back of the car.

We circled back to the drop, and he got out again. I went on to the parking area. We could not have asked for a better night. It was a frigid twenty degrees, and no windows were open, no dogs out. I parked and dropped the keys on the floor. I got out of the car and began to walk up the street I had just now driven down. I ducked between two homes, came out of the back, and made my way back to the wooded area. I made a little sound that we all knew, "Psst, psst," and Big G answered.

We met at the lookout, and he handed me a flashlight. We could see the main roads around the whole score. I guess it was around 1:00 a.m. We got a call on the scanner, but it was for the next town over.

It was 1:30 a.m., and here comes our boy, the local police. This was what we were counting on. He pulled into the station, proceeded in, stayed for about an hour, then came out and took off. We hung out until about 4:00 a.m., and he didn't come back. We knew we could do this. We wanted to be on the road as the five-o'clockers started on their way to work so we could blend in.

I went for the car, and Big G started on his way to the pickup spot. I picked him up, and we headed to the motel. I dropped off Big G and the tool bag, then went to grab some food for us. After that, we laid around all day, sleeping and watching TV. We didn't talk too much. I guess we both had a lot to figure out. We set the alarm for 11:00 p.m. again.

When it woke us up, we decided only to take the in-tool bag. We would leave the torch set in the room. We knew what we were seeking would not be in a safe. We thought it was in a closet or a lockbox. We checked everything and wiped it all off again. We put the tools in the trunk. We got into the car, and I pulled out of the motel onto the highway. This was one score we would remember all our lives.

We didn't talk. We knew where we had to go and what we had to do. We drove into town. Not much was going on in this small town around midnight on a Sunday. We got near the score, and everything checked out. We drove past. No one was around. We pulled over, Big G got out, and I popped the trunk. He got the tools out and got back in the car, and I pulled off. I then drove to the drop-off area. Big G hopped out with the tools, and I drove off to the sheltered parking area and parked the car. I then dropped the keys on the floor and stepped out. I scanned the scene—everything was perfectly normal. No crimes being committed here. I made my way through the houses up to the lookout area.

We met up at the same place we had met last night. Big G got some drivers out and handed me the radio and the hand scanner. He held onto his radio. We moved up to where we could see everything. Now, we watched and waited. It was about 12:45 to 1:00 a.m. We saw a few cars going by on the lower street. There was nothing going on with the scanner. Everything was in the norm around this small town.

We were about to step out of the norm, and I was feeling a little fucked up in my head. Here I was, going to B&E a police station for something that may or may not have been in there. But in a way, I was a little anxious to try this. I didn't know why, but this kind of thing does excite me. I was doing things that people only dream about. I would not ever do anything to hurt anyone, but finessing commercial burglaries was my thing.

Here comes the car we were looking for. It was about 2:00 a.m. The cop pulled into the station, got out of his car, and into the station he went. He was only in the station for about a half hour, and he came out, got in his car, and went off.

We decided to wait it out and make sure he didn't come back. It was a modest station house. It would not take us long to find what we were after. It was calm. Big G wanted me to stay where I was and be the lookout until he got to the station. We made our move.

Big G set off down the hill across the street and over to the station. He slid around the left of the station. There were about four windows on that side. He worked his way to the back window, where he broke into the station. He called me on the walkie-talkie and asked me for a green light. I gave him the go-ahead.

He said he would open the front door and to go to channel B on my radio. He unlocked the front door, asked me for a green light, and before going to move to the back door, he told me to go to channel C and come down. I made my move.

I hurried in the front door and locked it. As I came in, there was an office through one more door. Then, there were two more offices on the left side and two on the right, and a sizeable room in the back. We both started to shake down the offices, me on the left and him on the right. We were moving at a good pace and trying not to disturb anything. We didn't want anyone to know we were here.

We made our way to the back room. There was a huge, gray, two-door cabinet against the wall. This was the only place left that they would have evidence like the stolen gas mask from the firehouse raid. We opened the cabinet, and there was nothing there but paperwork.

I looked at Big G and leveled with him. "It's time to go."

I could see the look in his eyes. He was extra depressed at this time. We left out of the back door, and we didn't take anything at all. He headed to the pickup area with all the gear. I skipped out to get the car. We made our way back to the room. We packed up all the tools and our personal items, put them in the car, and off we went.

We didn't talk much as we drove back to Reading. We parked the car at the stash house. We got into our own vehicles, absolutely beat by this time. I was positively glad this was over.

Big G and I laid low for a few weeks. I went to work by day and would look for new scores by night every few weeks. And that was that.

CALLING MISS T, THE RAT'S EX-WIFE

I gave a call to the rat's ex-wife. She was excited to hear from me, and we made plans to get together. We partnered up for a few months and then fell in love. And I did love her, no bullshit. I moved in with her, and we were together for about five years. She and the rat had a little girl. I hated him with all my heart and still do. The reason I started to go out with her was to get back at him. And, let me tell you, in five years, I did.

MEETING RICK

Big G called me about two months after our trip to Clymer because he needed money for his attorney. Naturally, he wanted to go and make some. He told me there was someone that the boys from Allentown wanted us to meet. I thought that was cool.

We started going over our list. There were five clubs and a supermarket around the Jim Thorpe area. He wanted to go up there with the new guy and make our money, so we planned to meet again in a few days, when he would bring the new guy.

We both went back to our normal lives, and then I got a call—it was time to meet this individual. We had to go to Allentown and see our main boy, Pete. We all arrived at a mob-run restaurant at about the same time. Pete and the new guy were heading to the back tables as Big G, and I walked in. They sat down, and we joined them. Pete did the introductions around the table. After that, we all ordered drinks and dinner.

We made a little small talk through dinner. When Pete was through with his meal, he read Big G and me, considered the timing, and hinted that Rick, the new guy, would fit in with us. Pete explained that Rick was 100 percent man, and he would stand beside Rick no matter what.

"Okay?" he said, like we were supposed to agree with him. Pete was a big man around the Allentown area and north. He stood up and told us he had to leave, then asked us to give Rick a ride home.

Once Pete was gone, we informed Rick that we would give him a ride home after we talked and got to know him a little. We

59

took his number and said we'd give him a call, but he had to go to a few payphones and get their numbers. That's how we talked to each other—by bouncing around on the payphones.

We didn't want to spend too much time with him, just in case Pete had a tail on him. The FBI was on Pete now and then.

We paid the check, and I brought the car to the front of the restaurant. Big G and Rick got in. I asked Rick where to go. He wanted to drive to the other side of town. We talked a little about football and the weather. We knew better than to talk business until after we get to know him a little more. We dropped Rick off at his place and headed back to Reading. We talked a little about Rick and Pete on the way back home.

A few days passed by, and I received a phone call from Big G. We set a meeting up at the Chef's Lounge, and he said, "Rick will join us." That was our bar. We knew everyone that hung out there, a mixed crowd. It was home.

At the Lounge, we rehashed our plans for the coming Friday. We spoke to Rick about what we were into, and he liked our approach. I asked him what his forte was, and he said stickup man. I said, "We are not into that. We're commercial burglars. We like to outthink the normal situation, not hurt anyone, and take the money home."

He told us he was in.

We planned to go up around Jim Thorpe because we had a few A and B scores up there. We had to pick him up at his home on Friday. He said, "Fine." Then, we had some food, some drinks, and, I must say, we had a blast.

Friday came around. We got the work car and tools out of the stash house and headed up to Allentown. Halfway there, we stopped and called Rick from a payphone and instructed him to pack a bag. We picked him up a few blocks from his house and started to go over what we were going to do and what his job was. We told him he was going to be an inside man, helping me with the safe. We didn't want to put a new guy outside and trust him with something he had never done before. I would keep an eye on him.

We explained that we worked in Pennsylvania, New York, Delaware, Maryland, and New Jersey. These were the states where we made our money.

We made our way up to the Jim Thorpe area and drove by the clubs and the supermarket on our list. We all agreed on one busy club. Theoretically, it was an A+ score. We found the lookout area and some nice parking, then drove around and found a good drop-off area. We found what we needed to find and saw what we needed to see, so we left town and cast about for an adequate motel to stay at. We found a good one about one hour away.

SHOWING RICK THE ROPES

I showed Rick how we checked into motels, and we had no problems at this one. When you took out a fat wad of money and held it in your hand as you wrote down all the lies on the registry form, they didn't ask for ID.

I pulled out the keys to the room, and we brought in the tools. We showed Rick how to use the walkie-talkie and the hand scanner. After about an hour and a half, I felt he had got it.

It was Friday, and we had to wait until Sunday. We lit out for some food and a few beers, then back to the room. We would get up around 9:00 a.m. on Saturday and hit the road to peep more scores.

Come 9:00 a.m., we rolled out of bed, and off we went. We traveled north, and we found a few more scores to put on the list. I liked this Burger King, and I made a note to come back.

We were on the road for about seven hours, and it was time to head back to the room. We got back and cleaned the tools. We analyzed the plans a few more times and turned in for the night. We stayed in the room most of the next day because we didn't want anyone in the area to recognize us if the police came around and asked questions or showed any pictures afterward. I was not known as a burglar yet—only been busted for drugs up to now. Big G, on the other hand, was just coming off a bust.

We took naps and watched TV. At midnight, we studied the plan one more time. We exited to the car. Rick climbed in the backseat, and I got in the front. Big G drove out of the motel and headed for the score. An hour later, we passed the score, and everything looked flawless. We pulled over, so Rick and I could get the tools out. Then, we hopped back in the car with the tools, so when Big G came to the designated drop-off area, we could move in a flash.

He pulled over, and Rick and I hopped out. Big G took off to the parking area. He would drop the keys on the floor of the car and walk about six blocks to the lookout area to meet up with Rick and me. We were all feeling great about this score.

Big G took his position. Rick and I headed for the score. It was an easy in. In the back was a "popper" door. Well, you readers know what a popper door is—a round doorknob with a push button lock like you would have on your bedroom door that you could easily poke open from the outside. I scouted for a proper lookout place for Rick. I put him in place and checked for a second way out, as we always did. I found a side door. I then asked Big G for the green light, and he gave me an all clear. I yelled over to Rick and asked him if everything was sound. He replied, "Yes."

I started to shake down behind the bar. I found the safe in a little side room through a little side door. The safe had a small, square door.

"I found it," I said. "Better be on your toes."

He told me, "Okay."

I took a hammer out of the in-tool bag and knocked the dial off the safe. Then, I took a long punch out of the bag and hit the pin that held the safe door locks in place, driving it out of the way. I wiggled the handle on the safe door, but it didn't open. I hit the side where the pins were with the hammer and started to get movement. I love movement on a safe door. After a few more tries, the door came open.

I heard Rick asking for a green light, and we received one back. I heard Big G tell Rick to go to channel B, and I hurried to find a mop bucket. I put the money in the bucket and moved to the lookout area with the bucket and the tool bag. I gave Rick the tool bag and made him do the cigarette machine for the money and the smokes. I told him to do the jukebox, too. And this club had a one-armed bandit, a.k.a. poker machine. Almost every club had some type of illegal gambling going on.

Rick did the machines and put the money in the mop bucket. He put the cigarettes in a trash bag. I asked him to take over the lookout for a few minutes. I wanted to peek behind the bar one more time real fast. I'm glad I did, because I found a bank bag with the punchboard gambling money in it. I positioned myself at the lookout area, put the money in the mop bucket, and rolled it to the back door. Rick grabbed the tool bag.

I called Big G for a green light and signaled that we were ready to come out. He called back with a green light. We hustled out the door and made our way over to the outside lookout area.

Big G said, "Good job, boys," and went for the car.

Rick and I made our way over to the pickup area, and after about five minutes, Big G was there. He flashed the headlights high and low two times, so we knew it was him. We hit him with the flashlight two times. He pulled over, popped the trunk, and we were off.

We ran through how everything went beautifully. Big G told us we were only in there for about one hour. We did the safe, three machines, found the punchboard money, and shook the whole place down in one hour without any trouble.

We drove back to Rick's house in Allentown, where we laid the money out and started counting: about $4,500 in cash and $2,000 in change. We divided the money up, and Rick couldn't understand how we made that much in an hour. He was one happy man. Big G and I put our cash in our pockets, and Rick gave us some Tupperware for our change. We then notified Rick we would call him in a few days. Big G and I drove back to Reading. We put the car and the tools away, thinking Rick might not be that bad after all.

BIG G'S SENTENCING

Before we knew it, it was time for Big G to go to jail. We called it going back to college. He had to do about two and a half years for the Clymer job. At the same time, Little Joe was coming home.

When Big G shuffled into court for sentencing, the police brought up that someone broke into the station looking for something. Then, the judge asked what they did with the gas mask they had confiscated off Big G. The cop stated that they returned it to the station, so the firefighters could use it. When Big G told me this story, I just could not believe that they gave the mask back! When you have evidence for a B&E, you do not give it back so that people can use it.

Big G surrendered to do his time. After two years, he would get out on parole.

In the meantime, Duke, Rick, and I became a team. I had worked with Duke before, but only a few times. Plus, he knew Rick because Big G had hooked them up before he withdrew to jail.

I would still get a call from Little Joe now and then. He was running with Bill, and a few weeks or so after Big G's sentencing, he wanted to have a meeting. We met at the Chef's Lounge, and he wanted to know if I was working, and not a real job. He meant night work. I let on that I was just out looking around. I never tell on myself. He mentioned that he had a few things coming up.

I said, "You should give me a call."

We had a few beers together, talked about Big G a little, and then we went our separate ways.

THE GOOD MARKET

Duke called me, and we got together. He wanted to go out to Pittsburgh. We had a few places on our list from that area. He wanted to leave from his home around 5:00 p.m. Friday and bring Rick with us. It had been a little while since I did anything. I knew Rick and Duke had been working now and then, so I said, "Yes."

Well, Friday came, and we met. We jumped in Rick's work car. He and Duke had everything we would need. We drove six hours to Pittsburgh, found a room, and called it a night.

We set out to take in the sights in the little towns around Pittsburgh around 8:00 a.m. We checked the things we had on the list. We liked one club, but we kept looking, and after about four hours, we found the score we wanted to do. It was a supermarket in a real small town near Pittsburgh. It had a master safe, a Mosler, a tough one to get into, with a solid steel plate, square door on top, and round one on the bottom. It had no wires attached—no bugs, no alarms.

We rented a room about one hour from the score. It was a Saturday night around 5:00 p.m. We were thrilled that we had found this supermarket. It sparkled like gold. I couldn't wait for Sunday night to come.

We only stayed in the room all day Sunday. When night came, we brought the tools out and cleaned them. We broke the walkie-talkies out and programmed the scanner. We waited until around midnight to put the tools into the car. I was the driver, or wheelman. Most of the thieves I knew were dependable thieves, but they were no-driving fucks.

Near the score, I stopped. We set the tools out, and everything struck me proper. I dropped them off and parked the car. Then, I relocated to the lookout area at the front of the score while they headed behind the supermarket. I called them on the radio and said, "Green light." I could hear them trying to get into the market and had to tell them not to make that much noise. They said, "Copy that."

About ten minutes drifted by, and they told me they were in. They directed me around to the back. Rick would be the lookout until I found a way in.

I did as I was told. I entered the market and went to the front while Rick helped Duke in the back. I had an ideal lookout from where I stood.

They opened the square door in about one hour. They had to get the torch set out and burn the dial off the round safe. I could hear the torch going for the next hour and a half. When they finally opened the safe, I heard them say, "Holy fuck!"

I yelled, "What?"

They answered back, "We hit a big one!"

I asked if we were going to take the smokes.

They said, "No," and Duke made Rick get the car.

Duke told me to be on my toes as he was getting the tools and money to the back door and suggested I take a fresh look. I looked down, and there were two buckets packed full of cash. I thought, *There must be $20,000 in there.*

Rick came over the walkie-talkie from the getaway car and gave us the green light. Duke picked up the tools. I picked up the money. We both came out the back door while Rick was coming up the side of the supermarket. He almost ran over me.

Duke and I put everything in the trunk, and we drove out of there carefully.

Back at our room, we gathered our things, and then we hit the Pennsylvania Turnpike back to Reading. We drove to Duke's, took the buckets of money out of the trunk and into the house. Once inside, we poured the money on the floor. It took us about two hours to count it out—$47,000! This was the biggest score for me so far.

We cleaned up the tools and put them back in the car. On the way to the stash house, we stopped at a shop to mount some much-needed new tires on the car and throw out our old work boots. Duke and Rick took me home. We all laid low for a while. Astonishingly, in one weekend, I had made over $15,000.

CLUB NEAR ALLENTOWN

Well, Rick and Duke were not around. I didn't hear from them for a month or so. I received a call from Little Joe and Bill. They needed to make some money and wanted to meet with me. Joe asked me to come over to his home. When I got there, he and Bill were just bullshitting. I grabbed a beer out of the refrigerator and sat down with them.

They asked me how Big G was. I told them he was doing the best that he could in jail. They informed me they had something good for me to gander. "When?" I asked. Joe suggested we would go up and look on a Wednesday. "That's fine with me," I said. He wanted me to give him a call once I got off work around 4:00 p.m. I had a few more drinks and went home.

The next day, Little Joe came over to pick me up, and Bill was already with him. We hit the road to check this score. The ride took us about an hour. It was a VFW that had a carnival that weekend, and we were hoping that the money from the event would still be in the safe. It was an easy in—there was a popper door in the back.

We drove around and found parking and a drop-off area. We all liked the score and would come back on the weekend to make money. We all went home and waited for Sunday, and Sunday came real quick. When they picked me up in their car, they had the tools and radios with them. We would only use one car for everything.

We approached the score and drove around it. Again, everything looked perfect. We drove to an area where we could get the tools out, and I sat behind the wheel. They hopped out at the drop-off area, and Little Joe handed me a walkie-talkie. I drove off to the parking area, dropped the keys on the floor, and made my way over to the lookout area. Joe and Bill were there and asked if I was ready to do this. I said, "Yes. Let's do this."

They made their way over to the back door and came upon a house with a light on. So, they moved to a side window instead. It was unlocked, and they got right in. They asked me for a green light. I reported, "Everything is green."

After about forty-five minutes, I asked them for a radio check. They said they were okay. After forty-five more minutes, they asked me for a green light again. I gave them the all clear, and shortly after that, I saw them coming out of the club. They sent me to get the car, and that was that.

As I drove back to Reading, Joe talked about the score. The safe was on the third floor, and it was a small-capacity square body. It was easy to open, but there was not a lot of money in there. We made it back to Reading, and we hurried to Joe's house to count the money. There was about $2,500, so we all took our cuts and went our separate ways. Joe told me he would call me.

MOVING MY MONEY

Back in the '70s, I kept my money in a bank deposit box. I remember going to put money into it, and I couldn't get it all to fit. Around that time, I had heard the FBI was scrutinizing drug pushers using deposit boxes to hide drug money. I felt real nervous about that, so I took my money out and hid it in my house. That was it for putting money in the deposit box.

DIFFERENT CREWS

Remember, Big G was in jail yet, and here I was on parole, working with two different crews. I liked these guys, but I missed Big G. He and I worked flawlessly together. He was coming home soon, and I already had an ace score put aside for us to do.

Duke gave me a call. He and Rick wanted to have a meet on Tuesday night around 7:00 p.m. I told him I would be there. They wanted to make money. I had money, and I didn't need more, but I liked the excitement.

I showed up at Duke's right at 7:00 p.m. He let me in, and we walked back to his kitchen. Rick was there already. We said our hellos and got down to business. They wanted to chase a score up around Pottsville. I said, "I'm in, but want to try some kind of a fast-food score." They said that was cool, and we would gun for one. They wanted to meet on Friday at Duke's house around 6:00 p.m. I told them I would be there.

GETTING INTO FAST FOOD

Well, Friday night came, and Duke, Rick, and I headed up to Pottsville. We were on Route 61, about six miles south of Pottsville, going north, and in this little mall, I see a Long John Silver's. I told them to take a look, and they did with no huge response. I made a mental note. We drove into Pottsville, poked around. We saw a few clubs, but we didn't think too much of them. We headed up to Hazleton, looked around there, and saw a club and a supermarket we liked, so we rented a room up around Berwick and started to go over our notes. The three of us were not happy with what we had, so we called it a day and decided to talk about it tomorrow.

The next day, I made it known that I wanted to go back and prospect the LJS. They agreed. And if we liked this score, we could do it and stay in Reading overnight. It was only one and a half hours from home.

We left our room around 11:00 a.m. and headed back to look at the LJS. We didn't know anyone who had done one of these. We were the first to try one in our area. We reached the score, and the parking lot was practically full. We drove around, and there were no alarms that we could see. We scanned for parking and a drop-off area. We found what we needed, and we all liked what we saw.

We headed back to Reading, all went our separate ways and agreed to meet the next day at midnight. Little did I know that Sunday night was going to change the way I saw fast-food scores. I drove home and went to bed. I woke up Sunday and just hung out at home. Midnight came. I met with Duke and Rick, got into the car, and they reported that the radios and the other tools were ready to go.

We were on our way up to the LJS with Rick driving. We drove by. Everything looked to be favorable. We advanced down the road and took the tools out of the trunk, and Duke and I got back in. Rick drove to the drop-off area. He stopped. Duke and I got out and hurried to the front of the score. I didn't like what we had to do to get in through the front. I said to Duke, "Come on, let's go around to the side." We did, and on the one side of the score was a popper door.

Once I worked my way in, Duke and I ducked inside and turned on the lights. To our surprise, we were in the room where they kept the mops and mop buckets, and the mop buckets had wheels on them. I used them a lot, so it was good to know where to find them. I then took the sledgehammer off Duke, and we called for a green light. Rick came back with, "All green."

I started to punch a hole through the sheetrock with the sledgehammer, and really, it didn't take long before I came out in part of the kitchen. I scurried around to the office, and Duke found a lookout position. I knew that this place was not bugged, so I opened the office door and started to shake down the office. I saw a metal plate lying on top of the desk and picked it up. To my surprise, the architect for this fast-food place had put a mini, round-door safe on top of a cement slab. The slab was about twelve inches in diameter. The safe—about eight to ten inches wide and about three feet tall—was encased in cement—heavy duty.

Nevertheless, I tipped the desktop off, took my sledgehammer, and broke the cement away from the safe. I yelled, "Mop bucket!" to Duke, who was shaking down the front counter. A short while later, it was there. I put the safe in the mop bucket, and we made our way back to where we came in. I then asked for a green light, and Rick came back again, "All green." We slipped out the side door with the tools and the safe.

I rolled the mop bucket with the safe across the parking lot, and Duke had the tools. We made it to the lookout area and sent Rick to get the car. Five minutes later, we saw him coming down the road. He gave us the high beams and the low beams. We gave him the flashlight on and off. He pulled over, popped the trunk, and we threw everything in. Rick pulled away.

Now let me say this, if the architect would have put the round door safe into the floor, there's no way we would have gotten the money. It would have taken three to four hours to open the safe, and spending that much time in the hot zone for $3,000–$5,000 would not have been worth the risk. It only took us about one and a half hours to get in and come out with the money.

I also knew that if other Long John Silver's restaurants were laid out the same as this one, we could do these throughout the states we worked in. The only downside to riding around with a safe in your trunk was you had to find a place to open it, not to mention a place to dump it. I knew I would be focused on these LJSs from now on.

Now, we had to find a place to open the safe. We scrambled down the back roads toward Reading around 3:00 a.m. We passed this road going up a hill. We stopped and backed up the hill to where we could turn around. Once we were turned around, Duke and I got out while Rick popped open the trunk. We pulled out the cutting torch and the in-tool bag, then Duke and I pulled out the safe. We closed the trunk and turned on the walkie-talkies. We told Rick to give us one hour, and as he took off, I said to Duke, "I hope he can find us again," because Rick didn't know this area.

We had two flashlights out of the in-tool bag. While Duke started to put the torch set together, I began to mull over how we were going to open this safe. Where the manufacturer welded on the steel door was a good place to start. I took the torch set with oxygen and acetylene. I lit the torch and started to cut on one side in the middle of the weld, and, to my surprise, the weld cut easily. It simply melted out of the way. I was surprised one more time when the smoke cleared. There was a safe door-locking pin. We rolled the safe to the next side, and the same thing happened. And again on the third. Once that was completed, I took the punch and a hammer out of the in-tool bag. I gave each pin a few whacks, and we were able to pull the door off the safe

This was a night of surprises. We removed the bank bags, and they were full. We packed up the torch and rolled the safe down the hill into the woods. Then, we tried to get Rick on the radio. No luck. A few minutes later, we tried again, and we got a response: "Ten minutes." We moved down near the main road and saw a car. The headlights switched to high and then low, back to high and back to low. We knew it was Rick. Time to go. We turned a flashlight on and off to give him our location. He pulled up, popped the trunk, and off we went.

"How'd everything go?" Rick asked. We told him, and then he asked us, "How much money?"

I said, "Around $4,000 to $6,000."

He said, "That's great!"

We took off to Rick's house and all went inside together. I had the money with me. We divided the money. It was around $5,500, and that wasn't half bad for being in the hot zone for one and a half hours.

NO GUNS

We each took our cut of the Long John Silver's score, and to my surprise, Rick pulled out a small handgun, a .38 caliber, and laid it on the table. Then he looked at me, and I looked at him hard. My one rule was no guns. On top of that, it turned out Rick was an escaped prisoner. That's when I knew Rick and I would be parting ways very soon.

We called it a night, said our goodbyes, and Duke took me home.

On the drive, I told Duke I didn't like Rick having a gun when I worked with him. "Don't let it bother you," he said, and that confirmed it—I could only work with Rick and Duke a few more times, and that would be that. We pulled up, I got out, and on my way inside, I told Duke I would call him sometime.

THE JEWELRY SCORE

A month had passed by when I received a call from Little Joe. It was early Sunday morning. He gave me a payphone number and asked me to call him as soon as I could. I said, "One hour." I hopped out of bed. I was still living with Miss T, the rat's ex-wife. I let her know I would return in a few hours.

I found a payphone and called Little Joe in precisely one hour. He picked up and told me he was up in a little town near Harrisburg. He and Bill had broken through the floor in an apartment above a jewelry store on Saturday, and they could not get the safe open. He then explained that they could watch the jewelry store all day until I got there to open the safe. "This is a good score, and you could make a lot of money," he said to me. Then, he asked me if I was coming up to help.

I said, "I will." I asked if I had to bring anything. He needed me to bring more oxygen. I said, "No problem, but I need a call in two hours for an update." He told me that was fine.

It was around 11:00 a.m. I ran by my stash house, picked up the oxygen, and drove home. I started to speculate what kind of brute this safe could be that Little Joe could not get into it. I knew that Little Joe and Bill were hardcore B&E men and had done a lot more scores than I had. I laid my map out, looked for the town they were in, and found it—about two hours from my house. I tried to relax, but I couldn't. A lot was going through my mind.

Little Joe called around 5:00 p.m. and asked me if I could be up there between 8:00 and 9:00 p.m. He instructed me to drive down Main Street and watch for flashlight signals—off and on three times. Around 6:00 p.m., I was out the door. I rolled up to where they were around 8:20 p.m. I saw the signal on my first pass down Main Street. I rolled up to the next light, made a right, came down about three-quarters of a block, parked my car, got out, walked down to where I had seen the signal, and met Little Joe.

This town was dead. We took a little walk until we were standing across the street from the jewelry store. Bill was there, and we said hello to each other. He told me that everything was looking orderly. They had been there the whole time, and no one had come around. He then told me we could go in at any time. I still had to get the oxygen bottle out of my car. Joe gave me his walkie-talkie and said they would have the side door open.

I started walking. No one was driving around this town. I carried the oxygen as discreetly as possible and was back at the jewelry store in no time. I asked for a green light, and one came over. I walked over to the side door and went right in. Bill was at the window, glancing out. I walked behind the counter and over to the safe, where Little Joe was. I inspected Joe's work, where he had tried to burn the dial off this heavy, round door. I took a flashlight and gave it the once-over. I saw where he had attempted to penetrate the thick, steel box. I hooked up the oxygen to the torch set. I put my cutting glasses on, fired up the torch, and started to cut away.

About a half hour later, I had the dial off the safe. I turned off the torch. We let the smoke clear. I then took my flashlight and squinted. I could see the locking pins. I took the sledgehammer and hit the safe door. Two of the pins fell free, the top one and the side one. The bottom one didn't move. I pulled a light hammer and a chisel out of the in-tool bag. I saw that slag had fallen when I cut the dial off and was stopping the pin from moving. I put the chisel on the slag and gave it a whack. Off came the slag, and I hit the safe with the hammer and achieved movement.

I then moved the handle downward, and the safe came open. I started to pull the jewelry trays out, and Joe put the jewelry in duffel bags. I packed up the tools once the bags were full. Joe and I moved everything to the door we had come in. He let us know his car was across the street and up the alley. Bill came over to the door, and, when everything was clear, we all made our move. We walked to Joe's car and put everything into the trunk. We hopped in and left. They took me to my car, and before I got out, they told me to follow them. We drove back to Reading.

We put the hot car and the tools in the stash house and locked it down. We took the jewelry with us. We took off to Joe's with the jewelry and dumped it on his bed. It took them a few hours to go through it, about $100,000 worth. We would try to get about $35,000–$40,000 for it, Joe said, and he would make some calls and get back to me. I said, "Alright. Then you have a good night."

At that moment, I was thrilled about what had gone down in the last twenty-four hours.

I got home at about 6:00 a.m. on Monday, around 7:00 a.m. I called in sick to my job, and everything went back to the norm.

TRYING TO SELL THE JEWELRY

When Friday came around, I received a call around 6:00 p.m. from Little Joe. They wanted to have a meeting around 7:00 p.m. I said I could meet anytime. They said, "Okay, just go to Bill's."

When I got there, they were eating pizza, so I grabbed a slice and a beer and sat down. Joe got into how he and Bill wanted me to take the jewelry that we had stolen the other night to Pittsburgh and have a meeting with Frank the Fence, who I'd met a few times before when Big G and I journeyed to Pittsburgh to sell some smokes and other things we had gotten out of the drugstore scores. We would bring Frank goods and return home with money. He always had big money that he could get in no time. He was good pay.

I said to Bill and Joe, "I would be happy to go for the ride and see Frank." I then asked, "How much are we looking for?"

Their response was, "Do not to take less than $36,000."

"That would be cool. And, you know what? You just made my day."

They gave me Frank's phone number and address. We talked for about one more hour. Finally, Joe told me they had the jewelry in the trunk of the Cadillac. He had a new, 1977 Cadillac. It was a very cool car.

I left my car at Bill's, and Joe took me over to the Caddy. I told Bill I would be in touch, and Joe and I went on our way. I turned to Joe and said, "I need to stop at my house, pack a bag, and pick up my gun." I would take my gun on a trip like this. You never know what cards life will deal you at any time. You must be on your toes. I had $100,000–$180,000 in hot jewelry, I was going alone, and I'd be far from home.

Well, Pittsburgh was about five hours from my Reading place. I was on the road around 9:30 p.m., so I got in pretty late. I rented a motel room, took the jewelry out of the trunk, put my gun on the end table, and hit the sack. I knew tomorrow would be momentous.

I woke up around 10:00 a.m. Saturday morning, took a shower, checked in with Joe, assured him everything was cool, and said I would call Frank after I had something to eat. I put my gun in my belt, put the jewelry into the trunk of the car, drove to the diner around the corner, and parked my car where I could keep an eye on it. As I paid my bill, I asked for some change for the payphone outside.

Frank answered. He told me I would have to drive over to Beaver Falls. That was about thirty to sixty minutes northwest from where I was. I let him know I would call him when I got there.

I drove to Beaver Falls and gave Frank a call. He asked me to book a motel room and call him to let him know where I was. It took me another forty-five minutes to put the jewelry in the room and get everything together.

I called him again, told him where I was, and gave him the room number. He told me he would be there in one hour. I made it clear that I needed to see him and only him. He understood.

I tried to relax, but that didn't happen. Here I was, six hours from Reading, in a room full of hot jewelry, on parole, and with a loaded .45 caliber handgun on me.

The hour flew by, and a knock on the door came. I eyed through the peephole, and it was Frank. He was by himself. I opened the door, he walked in, and I took a long look around before closing the door. We said our hellos, and he asked to see the jewelry. I pulled the bags out from under the bed. I put them on top of the bed opened them up, and we examined the jewelry for about two hours. This was the first time I could see the jewelry laid out all nice and neat, and I liked what I saw.

I made it clear that Joe and Bill wanted around $36,000 or up, no less. I asked Frank if he liked what he was seeing. He told me he did, and that in a few months, he would have a jewelry store for us to do. Of course, I said, "Just let me know."

He said, "I'm going to call this guy named Paul. That's who you're here to see."

I said, "I would like for this thing to be over pronto, and tell Paul to come alone," and I put the jewelry away. Then, I let Frank out of the room and took one more glimpse around.

It was around 6:00 p.m. when I received a call from Frank. He had Paul with him. Frank put Paul on the phone asked if it was okay to come to my room in about thirty minutes. I said, "Okay," hung up the phone and called Joe. I relayed to him that Frank and I had examined the jewelry and that I had hung up the phone with

Frank and Paul a moment ago. I asked him if he knew Paul. Joe thought he had heard about him and added, "Be safe, man."

I said, "Okay. I'll call when I have some news."

When I heard that knock at my door, I took my gun off the end table. I looked out the peephole and didn't know the man out there, but I hoped it was Paul.

I opened the door but kept the chain lock on. "Who are you looking for?" I asked. He told me he was Frank's friend and was looking for Dale. I told him that was me, unlocked the door, and let him in. We said our hellos, and he asked to see the jewelry.

I let him see me put my gun in my belt around my back. Then, I fished the bags out from under the bed.

I sat on the other bed after putting my gun next to me and said, "Go ahead, take a look." As he studied the jewelry, he asked me if the score was around here. I let on that it was about five hours from here and a few weeks old. He gave me a little smile as he was going through the jewelry. He brought up some names of some people in Reading, and I knew most of them. He was putting some of the larger rings in a pile.

After about one hour of going through the jewelry, he asked me what we were looking for, and I went high—$47,000. I knew that he would try and work me down.

He countered, "I was thinking around $35,000."

"For that, I would have to make a call," I said, knowing once I talked to Joe, he would tell me to get the money and come home. Then, Paul said we had to go to his bar. I stood up from the bed, put my gun in my belt around my back, and started to put the jewelry away. He asked me if he could keep this one ring out. I said, "As long we come to an agreement with your price."

I put everything away, and I said, "I want to call Joe from the bar," and packed my things up. I was ready to go, because as soon as someone that I didn't know discovered what I had in this room, it was time to move.

I walked out to my car, and he went to his. I put everything in my trunk, but I kept my gun with me. And out of the parking lot we went. We drove about thirty minutes to a strip mall in front of an Italian shoe store. I parked my car beside his. We both got out, and he announced he was going to give me a present. He took the lead and walked into the shoe store. I was right behind him. He asked me what size shoe I was. I said, "Size ten." We walked over to the expensive shoes. They were about $200–$300 each. He instructed me to pick out two pairs of shoes. I picked out one brown and one black pair.

The girl that worked there walked over, gave Paul a little kiss on the cheek, and said hello to me. He asked her to put the shoes in a box and bag them. He didn't introduce us. She handed me the shoes. As we walked out the door, I said, "Thanks." And I must say, those Italian shoes were luxurious, very comfortable.

We headed to our cars, and Paul asked me to follow him. A few minutes later, we pulled up to this prominent bar and Italian restaurant called Good Times. The food was damn good, too. I parked my car so that I could see it from inside the bar.

Paul walked in. I stopped at the pay phone on the way in to give Joe a call. Joe asked me how things were going, and I said, "Good, so far. We are looking at around $35,000."

He said, "Make the money."

I told him I would call him back in a few hours, and he said, "Fine."

I walked into the bar. There were about fifteen to twenty patrons. We sat at a table, and Paul ordered us some food and drinks. He then walked behind the bar, picked up the phone, and made a call. He came back to the table and said, "I called my partner. He should be here in an hour or so."

The food came to the table, and we ate. Afterward, we moved to the bar. Paul introduced me to a beautiful woman behind the bar named Sandy. He then told me that she was his fiancée. Then, he proceeded to pull *my ring* out of his pocket and *proposed to her right in front of me*. As he was handing her the ring, she said, "Yes," and took the diamond ring from him with joy.

I, on the other hand, wasn't overjoyed about what had just happened. I thought he was taking the ring to show his partner the quality of the goods that I had brought to Pittsburgh. After all of this, I waited for the opportune time to ask Paul if he was going to purchase the goods. He told me to relax. He would call his partner again. After about an hour or so, I asked him again what was going on. I kept my eye on my car through the window of the bar. He told me that I would have to wait a little longer for him to make another phone call to his partner.

I know people. He was stalling. So, I decided to tell Paul to give me the number to the bar, and I would call him in an hour because I didn't like sitting in a bar with a trunk full of hot jewelry and a handgun on my person while on parole.

We said our goodbyes, and I headed for the car. I knew at the time that he was not interested. I climbed in my car and started driving south, heading home. Before I left town, I gave Little Joe a call and explained to him what had happened. He wasn't too happy about me losing one of the heftiest pieces of jewelry to

Paul. I was a little upset with him and said, "You sent me up here by myself to meet a person we don't even know. I was put in an odd position where I couldn't get the ring back." He wanted me to come home to Reading. By then, it was about 7:00 p.m. on Saturday.

I made it back to Reading at about 1:00 a.m. with no problems on the road. I gave Little Joe a call, and he told me to meet him at the stash house. We stashed the jewelry, we talked a little about what had happened, and then we said our goodbyes. I drove home thinking to myself, *Damn, this was a long weekend.*

Everything went back to normal life for me. I was back to work, and when Friday came, I received a call from Little Joe. He told me he had a present for me. I told him I would meet him at the Chef's Lounge at 9:00 p.m. He said, "That's cool."

When I rolled up, Little Joe and Bill were already there. I walked in and strolled to our table in the back. By the smiles on their faces, things must have gone well. Little Joe said, "Things went great."

The waitress walked over, and I ordered a round of drinks for them and Jack Daniels for me. After the waitress brought our drinks, Joe reached into his pocket and pulled out an envelope. He slid it across the table and told me my cut was ten thousand. That made me extremely happy.

I put the envelope in my pocket. We partied for a few hours, said our goodbyes, and went our separate ways.

ENOUGH OF RICK

Normal life lasted a month or so. Then, I received a call on a Tuesday from Duke and Rick. Duke said he would like to meet with me on Thursday. I said, "That is cool with me." He asked me to be at his house around 7:30 p.m.

He said, "Me and Rick are ready to make some money." I asked if they had anything planned, and he said that he had "a few clubs around Altoona."

I said, "I will be ready." I also brought up Rick carrying a gun on the scores that we had worked on, and how I didn't like that. He told me he would talk to Rick. He also reminded me that Rick was an escapee and was on the run. I said, "I don't like that either, but mostly the fact that he carries a gun." We talked for another half hour or so about unimportant issues and said our goodbyes.

Friday came around immediately. I called Duke around 5:30. He informed me that he and Rick would pick me up at my house around 6:30. They arrived at 6:30 p.m. on the dot, so I grabbed my bag and hopped in the car, which was a '73 or '74 former police car that Duke had purchased at a city car auction. We were on the road to Altoona, which was about two and a half to three hours away.

We grabbed a little motel room and brought in the hand tools, our radios, and our suitcases. We settled in. I pulled a pair of gloves out and put them on. I then took out the radio bag and the scanner frequency book. I went through the bag to see if we had the frequency chips for that area—we didn't. I said to Duke, "We will have to go to the nearest RadioShack." I wrote down the frequency number that we needed on a piece of paper. I then took the walkie-talkies out of the bag, wiped them down, and checked the batteries. Everything was alright, and I put all the radios back inside the bags.

I pulled out the in-tool bag, wiped all the tools down, and then put them back into the bag. Then, we got comfortable. Rick left to take a shower. That's when I asked Duke if he had that talk with Rick about the gun, and he said that he did. Duke and I then took our showers and called it a night.

The next day, we woke up around 10:00 a.m. We knew that RadioShack was open, so we stashed the tools in the closet, and I grabbed the one hand scanner to bring with us. We put the *Do Not Disturb* sign on the door, and I went and paid for another day. I told them that my friend was in there sleeping and to not disturb him.

Duke was already in the car when I got in, and we drove to RadioShack. I talked to the salesperson about finding the local police frequency, and I gave him the numbers. They had the frequency I needed. Then, I asked him for the state police frequency, and they had that, too. That made my day. Sometimes, we would have to go to a few RadioShacks before we found what we needed.

I made my way back to the car. I got in and told Duke they had everything. That made him happy. We drove back to the room to pick up Rick. He was ready to go. We all climbed into the car and drove to the northwest side of Altoona. Duke had two clubs in that area that he wanted me to feast my eyes on: an American Legion club, and a Veterans of Foreign Wars.

We rolled up to the area and found the VFW. We drove around it. It was a B club, but very doable. We then proceeded over to see the American Legion, which was a fifteen-minute ride away. We drove around this club, rated it a C, and decided to go up Route 36 West to Patton, which was about another twenty minutes. We didn't see anything there that we liked, so we headed south over to Nanty Glo. There was a nice supermarket there that we wanted. All three of us got out of the car, went in at separate times, and walked around the store. It was a medium-size place. The safe was a round-door/square-door combination, like the one we did in Pittsburgh. This was better, and we found our score for the night. We looked for a drop and pickup spot, a parking spot, and then we drove around to try and familiarize ourselves with the area. After a few hours, we headed back toward the room. We stopped to get some food to go. It was Saturday, around 6:30 p.m.

We were good to go on Sunday night to do this supermarket score. We lay around all night Saturday until Sunday around 10:00 a.m., I paid for the room for one more day, and we went north from Altoona to survey for something we could put on the list for the next time we were in the area. We passed through Bellwood, and nothing was exciting there. We headed to Tipton, nothing there. We traveled a little more north to Tyrone. We found a VFW and a supermarket that we liked, and we put them on the list, headed back to the room, made it back around 4:00 p.m., ate again, and relaxed for a while.

Before we knew it, it was midnight and time to go to work. I took my driver's license out and left my wallet in the room, and so did Duke. Rick didn't even have any ID. I pulled a pair of gloves out, grabbed the radio bag out and the in-tool bag, and got into the car. I would be the driver. We headed toward Nanty Glo and got there about 1:00 or 1:15 a.m. We drove past the supermarket, drove around so we could get the tools out, and on the way, we passed a local police cruiser. He gave us a really hard look. We decided to drive out of town and let the local police gather that we were just passing through. After forty minutes, we decided to make another pass. As we were coming back into Nanty Glo and getting close to the supermarket, don't you know it—we passed *the same cop*. He took another hard look at us and made a U-turn. He pulled behind us and put his lights on, pulling us over. I turned around and told Rick to be cool. I would handle this.

He asked me for ID. He gave the evil eye to Rick and Duke in the backseat, then at me, again. He was such a young cop. He asked what we were doing in the area. I said, "We're just passing through and heading to Penn State to see my family up there." You could sense the tension in the air. You could almost cut it with a knife. I thought that at any minute, Rick was going to shoot this cop. The cop also felt that something was funny. He glared at Rick in the backseat again, and then at me.

He said, "As long as you are heading out of town, that is fine with me." He handed me back my license. "Go ahead and leave."

I realized that this weekend was shot because the cop knew my name. I also decided that my and Rick's partnership would be over soon. I knew that if something happened, Rick would have a shootout with the police, and I didn't want any part of that. So, we drove back to the room to get our shit and get out. We all knew that we were incredibly lucky because even though the cop was young, he wasn't stupid.

To this day, I think that cop knew something was going on. It was about 3:00 in the morning and no one was around but three bad-looking men up to no good. Not much was said on the way to the motel. We collected our things and headed back home.

No one talked a lot on the way back to Reading, either. Duke and I dropped Rick off, and that's when I said to Duke, "I would think hard about going out with Rick again."

Duke didn't say too much. He and I were not too tight. He didn't like how fast I had learned the B&E business.

TAKING A BREAK

Everything returned to normal for a few weeks. I received a letter from Big G. He wrote that things were going okay and asked me to send some money. Big G wrote to me about three times a month. I was happy to hear from him. Life was not the same without him. I would send him whatever he needed. I didn't suspect that the cops knew about me yet. I felt I had a favorable edge over them because of that, so when I received a call from Duke asking if I wanted to go to work, I told him I was going to take a break. He was not too happy about that. I also said that I would call him when I was ready to go out again. We said our goodbyes. I would have to do some thinking about if I would go to work with Rick again.

I took off from night work for a few months. I went out dancing and drinking and having a good time. Eventually, I called Little Joe, and we met at the Chef's bar. We had a few drinks, and he asked me if I was doing anything yet. I asked him if he had work for me. He said he did, and we would get together again to talk more about it. I said that was cool. He had a few more drinks and confessed that he had to meet a little honey. I asked him if I knew her. He only smiled and drank his drink, and out the door he went.

THE YORK JOB

Everything was great at my job, and my life was a happy one. I received a call from Duke. He wanted to have a meeting with me. I told him to meet me at Chef's Lounge on Friday at about 9:00 p.m.

Friday came around real fast. I showed up around 8:30 p.m. that night. I knew about everyone there and had a few drinks with a few of the regulars. It was getting close to 9:00 p.m., so I moved to our regular spot. A few minutes later, Duke came in. He walked to the bar, ordered a drink, took a sip, gave the place the once-over, and made his move to our table. We said our hellos, and he got right down to business.

He asked me what was wrong with working with Rick. I then asked him if he was drinking a lot. He eyeballed me and said, "This is my first drink of the night."

I then said, "Rick is an escaped convict. He always carries a gun, and to me, that means trouble. Listen, Duke. We made money with Rick, but sooner or later, our luck will run out, and some bad things will happen."

Duke understood where I was coming from. He then said, "Rick is a one hundred and ten percent guy to work with." At that time, I knew that no matter what I said, Duke was with Rick, so I asked him what he had in mind. "Me and Rick found a supermarket up around York. It does healthy business and has the Mosler safe, and we know how to work those." Then asked me if I was in. I asked him how long I had to weigh this job before I would have to give a yes or no. Duke looked at me, "You have to let me know soon, like in a few days." He drank his drink, stood up from the table, and told me he would call me.

Days can feel like minutes. Wednesday night, I got the call, and Duke asked me if I was in our out. I said I was in. He wanted me to be ready Friday night, and he would pick me up at my house around 7:00 p.m. I replied that I'd be ready, and Duke pulled up on time. I gathered my overnight bag, walked over to the car, and he told me to drive.

I got in the driver's seat after putting my bag in the trunk. I said hello to Rick. He said hello back, but, I guess by now, Rick figured that I didn't like to work with him and his time with me was coming to an end. He knew that I knew he was packing, and if some shit went down, he would use the gun and not think anything of it. He and I simply could not communicate like we used to.

I guess by now Rick knew that I didn't like to work with him because I knew he was packing a piece. If some shit went down, I knew he would use the gun and not think anything of it. After about two hours, we were up around the score. Rick rented the room. It was around 10:30 p.m. We ate and got comfortable. Me and Duke put the map out and started to go over what we were going to do on Saturday. After talking for an hour or so, we called it a night. It was February or March, and it was bitterly cold out.

We began moving around 10:00 a.m. I went out for some coffee and food. We ate, paid for the room until Monday, and off we took for the day. We put the sign on the door—Do Not Disturb.

We drove up to Carlisle, sightseeing for scores up in that area. After a few hours of driving through some small towns and not finding any respectable jobs to do, we headed down to the supermarket. We drove by and turned around. To me, at first look, it was no more than a so-so score. It had two other stores beside it: a pizza place and a shoe store.

I pulled up to the business and parked. Rick went into the pizza place. Meanwhile, I exited the car and headed into the supermarket. There were not too many people in the store for a Saturday. The safes were up front, a round door on top of a square door. I didn't see any alarms, and nobody noticed me while I was walking around. I liked this score.

When I got back to the car, Duke and Rick were ready to get out of there. I started the car and drove around behind the mall. There were woods about a hundred yards away. Duke asked me how I liked it. I said, "It's just so-so," but I drove around to the street, and after an hour, we found some alright parking and a good drop-off area. We struck out around the nearby towns looking for more scores, didn't see anything we liked, and then ordered some food and headed back to the room. We stayed in the room for the rest of the night. Sunday morning, we went out, ate, came back, and quietly waited around until 10:00 p.m. Then we broke out the tools, wiped them down, and checked them out again. We made sure that everything worked, and it did. We put the tools in the trunk of the car and the Do Not Disturb sign up. The stage was set.

I sat in the driver's seat, Duke rode up front, Rick climbed in the back, and off we went. Little did I know the circumstances of that night would affect my life in many different ways.

I drove past the score. Everything looked right. I drove to the drop zone, and that seemed good, too. I pulled over and popped the trunk. Rick and Duke got out and grabbed the tools. Duke came to the driver's side to hand me a walkie-talkie. Then, they both disappeared into the night, and I returned to the parking area and started to make my way to the back of the supermarket. I found my spot, but there was no Rick or Duke. I called them on the walkie-talkie and asked where they were. Duke came through and explained that they were in the supermarket. I told him we didn't work like that, because, if something had happened, I would have stumbled right into it, and that would not have been good. "We wait for everyone to be there before we make our move."

I was pissed, but I told him I was out back now and waiting for the green light, and Duke said to give him a minute. So, I sat out back in the woods while they got their shit together. Now remember, I was about one hundred yards from the back door of the supermarket. Finally, I got the green light from Duke. I let them know I was heading over, he said, "Okay," and I started to run. About five hundred feet into the run, I heard a car coming down the side of the supermarket, and it was coming fast. I knew who it was—the police!

I turned to my left, and there was a green dumpster. I thought that if I could make it to the dumpster, I could move around it as they were driving by. I barely made it to the dumpster and jumped behind, but to no avail. They saw me, but just before that, I was able to take my cloth gloves off, fold them into each other, and throw them into the dumpster with the walkie-talkie. I heard the walkie-talkie slide to the bottom of the trash, and the cops didn't see me do any of that. Thank you, God.

There were two policemen in the car. They stopped the car in front of the dumpster and ordered me to come out with my hands up. I did as they asked, and they put me on the hood and frisked me. They asked me what I was doing in the back of this mall. I told them that my friend and I were drinking around here, we had a fight, and he threw me out of his car. They put the handcuffs on me and started to search around and inside the dumpster. They pulled out the cloth gloves. Immediately, they shined the flashlight on my hands to see if there was any residue from the gloves.

When I threw the gloves in the dumpster, I wiped my hands on my pants, and when they shined the flashlight on my hands, there was no residue. I recall folding the gloves into each other was a valuable help, too.

They put me into the police car and started to drive around the building, shining their imposing light on all the doors and inside the windows. They did this two times, and they didn't see anything. Then, they drove to the police station. I gave them my name and where I lived, and they put me in the cellblock.

I knew that Duke and Rick would pull out of the supermarket because that was one of our rules: if one of us goes missing, we pull back and find out what happened. I knew the police were checking the market out while I was sitting in the cell. After about three hours, the cops that had picked me up came to my cell and informed me they were going to let me out. I asked them where the bus station was. The one officer said he would take me to one.

At this time, I didn't trust anything, because I didn't know what went down with Duke and Rick. I could only hope that they pulled out of the supermarket job when I didn't come to the back door. I knew they saw the police going around the supermarket, checking it out.

The officer took me out of my cell and told me to come with him. We exited through the back door of the station and got in his car. He put me in the backseat. He drove me to the bus station and let me out. It was about 3:30 in the morning, and it opened at 10:00 a.m. After I got out of the car, the cop parked down the street and kept an eye on me.

Well, after about thirty minutes, I started to hitchhike out in front of the bus station, and the first car that came by stopped and picked me up. My luck was so super. It pulled over, and I hopped in. The car was full of bikers who were drunk as hell. I thought I was going to die. I started to tell them about the bikers that I knew in Reading. To my surprise, they knew some of them. They asked me where I was going. I told them that "right here" was good. I was a few miles out of town, and the cop hadn't followed us. They stopped the car, and I got out. I was so glad to be out of that car.

Now I would have to be on my toes if the cops saw me again. If they picked me up once more, I would be in big trouble. I made my way back to where I had parked the car, and it was still there. No one was in the area, thank God. Duke and Rick must have been having trouble getting back to the car, or they got busted. I picked out a place where I could watch the car and no one could see me.

About a half hour wasted away, and here comes Duke and Rick. I asked them what the fuck went on. They explained how they did the safe, and there was no money in it. I didn't believe them. I asked why they did the safe without everyone being there. They told me they thought I got spooked. I said, "I got picked up and was in jail. And you guys just put a lot of heat on me." They said they thought we would need all the money we could get. I told them to go fuck themselves and to take me home, and we didn't talk at all. We pulled up to my house, I gathered my things, and I told them to go fuck themselves again.

I was done with them. What those assholes did was let the cops know that I was one of the men going around opening these safes. Things would never be the same. I would have heat on me for a long time because of this. I had some money stashed, and I always worked, but I also knew Duke and Rick would have a hard time trying to find someone that would work with them.

PUTTING DUKE IN HIS PLACE

After a month or so, some rumors started to go around about me that I had lost my heart for the B&E biz. I knew that Duke had started this bullshit. He was out of money and trying to get someone to work with him. Now remember, this was in the late '70s, and everyone wanted to be someone back then. I really wanted to make money and do out of the norm things to get it. I didn't showboat or buy too many new clothes or jewelry, and I didn't like any bullshit or heat in my life.

One day, I was working at my job, and Duke came over to my house, drunk, and told Miss T, the rat's ex-wife, that he wanted to talk to me. When I got home, Miss T gave me the facts of what happened. I went to my bedroom, grabbed my gun, checked it out thoroughly, put it in my belt, got in my car, and drove to Duke's house.

I knocked on his door. He opened it, and I asked him what he wanted with me, and then he called me a few names and took a swing at me. That's when I started to fuck him up real, real bad. I beat on him for about ten or fifteen minutes. I had to stop myself because if I didn't, things could have gotten out of hand. Then, I opened his door, threw him on the floor of his house, and said, "Stay away from me and my family. Understand?" He said, "Yes, I understand you."

I said, "You better. And go fuck yourself." I left. I headed back home, put my gun away, and carried on with my life, and about a month passed by with no problems. I heard a little shit from Big G, Bill, and Little Joe for what I did to Duke, but that was it.

Then, one Saturday afternoon around 1:00, there was a knock on my door. I looked out, and there was Duke. I told Miss T to go to the door but not open it—just talk through it.

I charged out the back door and came up behind Duke. I grabbed him and threw him down on my porch. He was drunk. I patted him down to see if he had a gun. Lucky for him, he didn't. That would have really pissed me off. I threw him off the porch and said, "Get out of here before you get hurt bad." I made it clear to him I would by no means work with him or Rick again. I said, "You and Rick put a lot of heat on me with that market job, and I'll never get over that." I threw him in his car. He didn't say anything as he drove off.

After the market job, the cops did follow me around for a little while. But I knew that they couldn't do that for long because they didn't have the resources. I couldn't do anything for a few months.

BILL'S MURDER

Bill worked at this beer distributor for a few years. One night while he was closing, somebody shot him two times from about 160 yards away with thirty-oh-six rounds. The first bullet hit him in the stomach and spun him around, and the second one hit him in the chest. When he hit the ground, he was dead. When I heard what happened, I figured one of the safe companies had put a hit on him. If a safe company lost money because burglars were opening their safes, I had heard, they would put a hit out. I was also told stories that if the cops could not catch you, the safe company would take care of it themselves.

Some people thought a mad father had killed Bill. He was going out with a young girl that lived a few doors down from the beer distributor. When the father found out, he went off. The cops interviewed him a few times. He was a hunter and had a lot of guns, but they didn't arrest him. In my heart, I felt that Bill was killed because of the heavy safe jobs my crew and I were doing. I'd seen the girl's father, and, to me, he didn't look like the type that could do this type of thing. No one was ever arrested for this crime.

Everyone attended the funeral. Duke and Rick rode together. Rick pulled me aside and said, "Duke is sorry for what he did." Rick also apologized and asked if he could call me.

I said, "That's okay."

We put Bill in the ground, and I went home.

Bill, rest in peace.

THE GOLDSMITH JEWELRY SCORE

It had been about four months since the supermarket job, I hadn't done anything except for my regular day job, and I was ready to make some money. I needed money to make money. I had made a ton of hard cash up to now, and I did not party it all way or spend it all on new clothes. For cars, I'd get my friends to drive me where I wanted to go. I hid and lived out of motels while out doing jobs, to keep the heat off me as much as possible. I lived comfortably and took care of my family, but getting good at commercial burglary required cash flow to keep working.

About a week after the funeral, on a Thursday, I received a call from Rick. He told me he'd received a call from Frank the Fence in Pittsburgh. Rick wanted to go up there. He said, "It will only be me and you, no Duke, and that will give us time to talk."

I told him, "That would be fine."

We agreed that he would pick me up on Saturday around 9:00 a.m., and Saturday morning came lickety-split. Rick was on time, he popped the trunk, and I put my bag in. We were just going to look at the score, no tools. He asked me if I wanted to drive.

"Sure," I said and sat behind the steering wheel. Off we went. About an hour into the drive, Rick asked me if I was still mad at him and Duke.

I said, "Yeah, I'm pissed off at Duke because I had to put him in his place two times, and I don't like the heat that was brought on me from everything that occurred at the last market job."

Rick told me that people make mistakes in life. Then, he changed the subject.

We stopped and grabbed something to eat. There was no more talk about Duke or work. We just talked about the weather and pussy.

When we got up to Pittsburgh around 3:00 p.m., we called Frank. He asked us to come up to Beaver Falls and meet him at the mall—just call him once we got there. Rick told him we were about forty-five minutes away.

We drove to the mall, Rick gave him a call, and Frank said to stay put, and he would be there in fifteen minutes.

Later, we saw him strutting over. We both said hello. He told us to come take a ride, and we drove north for about twenty minutes. There was the next score, a large jewelry store that was supposed to have a lot of gold bars. Frank explained to us that this could be worth about a half-million dollars. He explained how the cop who worked the night shift at this mall would come to the back door and let us go if something went wrong.

He said, "One of you will have to meet this cop." Apparently, Frank had a diagram of how to get inside the jewelry store without setting off the alarm. I asked Frank how long he'd known this guy.

"About fifteen years," he said. He mentioned that he had done things with him before. At that point, Rick and I agreed to meet him.

I still didn't like anyone knowing who I was and what I did, and I didn't like being the hero, but I utterly loved making six or seven figures. We drove around the jewelry store. There was a pizza place on the one end of this little mall, an art gallery and a studio in the center, and then the jewelry store. I saw the alarm box on the front of the store. It was a local alarm. I had worked them before with Big G.

I told Frank to park at the pizza parlor. Rick ordered a slice while I wandered past the art gallery and gave it the once-over—it wasn't bugged. I walked into the jewelry store and looked around. There was a heavy-duty, square-door safe; I could open this type very fast. There were alarm sensors on the front door, the back door, and on the air conditioner.

They had a lot of authentic jewelry on display. I gave the store another look, then said goodbye and thanks to the lady that was helping me.

I hurried to the car, and Frank started to drive. Rick asked me what I'd seen, and I filled them in.

"The safe's no problem," I said. That made everyone happy. Frank told us he'd drive back to where the car was parked. Then, he'd call the cop to see if he was available.

We got back to the mall and went straight to the payphone. Frank got in touch with the cop, and he wanted to meet. I stayed at the mall while Frank and Rick went. After about two hours, they returned. We said our goodbyes to Frank, told him we would be in touch with him soon, and Rick and I walked out to the car. Rick suggested we get a room near the mall.

At the hotel, Rick let me know me what the cop had said: "The best time to do the score is on a Sunday night, because the art studio might have someone up above the store working late on Saturday." The cop told Rick that he would come to the back if something went wrong and would let us go.

I went over the diagram and understood it. We would go in the art studio, and from the back wall, we would measure ten feet and punch a hole into the jewelry store. That would hopefully keep us clear of any alarms and put us about five feet from the safe. The cop must have been in the two stores a few times.

It was Saturday night, so we rested up, agreeing that the following night, we would go down to the jewelry store and observe it thoroughly in the nighttime. We grabbed a bite to eat and went to sleep.

We woke up around 10:00 a.m. We paid for the room, in case we found ourselves tired and needed to rest for a little while. Then, we found some food and headed north of Pittsburgh to look around for some more night work. We found some things that looked good, but that's another story.

We headed back to the room around 6:00 p.m. Rick brought up who we would bring to help us on this job. We talked about Danny B., Little Joe. Big G was in jail yet. And then, he mentioned Duke. One thing about Duke was that he knew what to do in this type of score. He had the right experience. Rick also put it out there that we would have to decide later, so we took it easy until around 11:00 p.m. Then we got underway, leaving everything in the room. We stopped for some gas and some coffee, scoped drop-off and parking areas, and drove by the score—standard practice to make sure it was clear and safe for use to begin.

The pizza place was closed, and there were no cars in the parking lot around back as we drove through it. To our advantage, two of the three lights were out in the parking lot behind the jewelry store. Everything looked terrific, so we drove out of there, and no one saw us. If we'd had tools, we would've done it that night. Oh, well. If I could see the future, I wouldn't be a thief.

Everything lined up well for the next weekend, but me, not thinking, authorized Rick to bring Duke. I saw a little smile on Rick's face. He said he would talk to him, and I added, "Make sure that Duke understands that I don't want any shit from him."

"I'll tell him," Rick said.

This was a big score, and they didn't come around too often. I could walk away with a hundred grand or so. I wanted people who knew what they were doing on this one.

Back in the room, we slept until around 9:00 in the morning. Then we hit the road, and six hours later, we were back in Reading. Rick pulled up to my place and popped the trunk, so I could get my equipment out. He said he would get back to me about Duke. I got out, told him to call, grabbed my things, and went into my home.

Well, it was Monday now, and I missed another day at work as a shipping supervisor. Rick told me he would drive for a few hours, and then I could take over from there. I said, "That's fine."

Rick called me later that week and notified me that Duke was in and that he'd pick me up around 5:00 p.m. on Friday.

Friday at 5:00 p.m., Duke and Rick were at my home. I moseyed out, put my gear in the trunk, and they had all the tools. I got in the car, and Duke and I exchanged greetings. He was acting like an intelligent human being, not a drunken asshole, for a change.

We talked about the weather and other non-work-related things. Rick drove about three hours, and then I drove to the north side of Pittsburgh. We chose a different motel than last time. Duke rented two rooms on the first floor. We backed the car up to the rooms side by side and brought everything into one place. I told them I would take the room with the tools because I was a smoker, and they didn't smoke.

There was a door between the rooms, so we could work together until we brought everything inside. Around 11:30 p.m., I told everyone I was going get some shuteye. I had worked all day, driven three hours of a six-hour drive, and I was tired. I asked them to get me up when they got up. We said our goodnights.

I thought about Duke for a few minutes that night. Thankfully, he didn't cause any trouble.

They woke me up around 9:00 Saturday morning, and we went for something to eat. After leaving the diner, we took the hour drive to the score so Duke could see it, and we filled him in on everything as we drove past the score. Everything looked the same. I could not wait to do this score, but the cop had told us the best night to do the score was Sunday, so we headed back to the room to discuss what we all had in mind.

Once we all got inside, Rick opened up that he wanted to do the score tonight. Duke said the same thing, despite the cop's advice for Sunday night.

"If we have some kind of problem with the safe, we could have more time to work on it on Sunday because the jewelry store won't be open," Rick reasoned.

I remembered that my friend Little Joe once had some trouble with a jewelry store and needed more time, so I had to agree with Rick. We all decided to do the score that night, and now, we had to check out all the tools and make sure we didn't need anything, and we had them wiped, organized, and in the trunk by around three. We decided to kick back until 11:00 p.m.

I strolled around and bought some food and a newspaper. We would always check out local papers to see if anyone was doing the same night work as we did. This time, there was nothing in the press. We ate, and I went back to rest in my room. Eleven came around, and Rick woke me up. It was time to go and make the money, hopefully. We put our bags in the car since we would not be coming back this way. I hopped behind the wheel, and once Duke and Rick got in, I drove off.

At the score, everything appeared to be in order. I drove past the drop-off and pulled over. Duke and Rick jumped out and grabbed the tools from the trunk, then hopped back in the car. Rick gave me a walkie-talkie and the scanner. I drove to the drop-off area, pulled over, and then Duke and Rick disappeared into the night. I parked the car with no problem and snuck over to the lookout area, where they were standing.

We stood there for about ten minutes to get the feel of what was around us. The plan was that Duke and Rick would get the "in" at the back door of the art studio, and we would go through the wall into the jewelry store.

We made our move. Rick and Duke breezed right in the art studio, and Duke tiptoed to the front to be the lookout so I could come across the parking lot and into the store. They called for a green light over the walkie-talkie, and I gave it to them. I made my move. Everything was going great. I made my way in the back door, broke the diagram out, and paced off the distance from the rear wall. I measured from the floor up to where we were going to put the hole, then grabbed a hammer out of the bag and hit the wall—all sheetrock.

After two or three whacks, I made a small hole into the jewelry store. After about twenty minutes, I was able to climb in and view the score. The alarm did not go off. We were in, and I could smell the money.

A two-by-four was in the way. I picked up the hammer and gave two whacks. Then, we heard someone up above in the art studio—a stomp on the floor. That was it. Time to get the hell out of there, because we knew the cops were on their way. I could not believe what had just happened. I was *in the jewelry store*, and the money was *right there*.

We grabbed up all the tools and made our way over to the parking area. We threw the tools in the trunk and jumped into the car. By now, we could hear sirens. We slid down in our seats and parked about ten minutes' walk from the score.

The cops searched up and down the streets. They only came by where we parked once, and they were shining their lights all over the place. We just sat there for about two to three hours. It was March, and it was cold.

Finally, I sat up behind the wheel, started the car, and drove off using a back road.

After a few hours on the road, I told Rick and Duke I was glad that whoever was upstairs banged on the floor. I knew Rick had a gun on him, and things could've gotten real ugly.

We made it back to Reading, back to my home. I popped the trunk, got out, grabbed my bag, and told them I would call them. Rick got in the driver's seat and sped off. They both called a few times. My girl took the message, but I didn't call them back.

Eventually, they stopped calling.

• • • • • • • • • • • • • •

PART III

TIME FOR A NEW JOB

By 1977, I became bored with the shipping job, and they didn't want to give me any more money. I took a second shift job at General Battery, making lead dioxide for their battery plates. My title was furnace operator. I worked in a sweltering environment. We had to wear two pairs of clothes every day and a mask that would keep the lead smoke out of our lungs.

They fed the furnace from the upper floor. The metal would melt down to where I could take a long, steel-handled ladle, dip out the lead, and put it in a steel mold. I'd stack them up, and the forklift operator would pull the pile out of the way so we could make more lead ingots. Every hundred or so, they would grab a bar and test it for high lead content. If the metal didn't contain the level they wanted, they would re-melt it until they formed it right.

They would also test us for high lead levels. They would take a blood sample every two weeks and do the test in the nurse's office. She would tell us if we had high levels of lead. If we did, they would let us do some other kind of work. I made decent money at that place. It was a good job, I worked there for about four years, but like with any job, eventually, routines get boring.

OPENING TWO SAFES

After not doing anything for three or four months, I received a call from Rick. It was about 3:30 a.m. on a Sunday, and I hadn't talked to him for a long time. He laid it out that he and Danny needed my help opening two medium, round-door safes. Apparently, they'd gone up around Pittsburgh, grabbed a car, and done two fast-food places. But they threw the safes in the trunk and drove them back to Reading because they knew I could open them without burning up the money inside.

Remember, money does not come free. I asked Rick what was in it for me. He and Danny agreed to give me one third. I couldn't pass this opportunity up. They had done the hard part, getting the safes out without getting busted, and there was no local heat for these burglaries. This was a piece of cake.

They thought I would need my cutting set, which was hidden down at the boat works at a friend's cabin. I knew right where they were and said I would arrive in half an hour. I woke up Miss T and made her get ready because she would have to drop me off. I didn't want my car around there, just in case something happened. I told her I had to help someone out. She glowered at me and said frankly, "Yeah, okay," so I went down to the basement, grabbed the two torch bags, and then put them in the trunk. Miss T and I were out of there in no time.

The cabin was about ten minutes from my house. She dropped me off with the bags. She couldn't tell what was in them, but she knew whatever I was doing, it was on the shady side of the law. There wasn't another cabin within a mile. I knocked on the door. Danny answered, and I walked into the living room and saw they had the two safes sitting on a piece of steel from an old heater, ready for me to get to work. I arranged my gear, fired up the torch, and started to cut along the weld.

Safe companies weld the top part and the door connector to the safe. By cutting a hole in the weld on three sides, about three inches in diameter, I was able to wiggle the door and see the locking pins move. I took a punch and a hammer, hit the door locks in, and pulled the door off the first safe. I let Danny and Rick pull the money out, and I started to work on the other safe. It was open in no time, but, even with the windows open, there was a lot of smoke in the room. After letting it clear out, we divided the money up. I made around $2,000 in about two and a half hours and didn't even sniff the hot zone.

It was summertime, so it was already starting to get light out. Rick asked me if I would help them dump the safes in the river. I needed a ride, so I said I would. I put my torch and bottles back in their bags, shoved the money in my pocket. We loaded the safes in the trunk, and it was time to dump them in this river that was right there, about five blocks from the cabin. Rick got in the driver's seat, and Danny rode in the front, while I was in the back.

We picked out a spot, and Rick pulled over. Danny and I got out. Rick handed us the keys to open the trunk. I gave the keys back to Rick. We lifted one of the safes out, slogged about three feet into the water, and tossed it. We slogged back to the car and started to hoist the other safe out when suddenly we heard a car coming up the road fast. We turned around. *Here comes a fucking cop.* I couldn't believe it. I gave a yell out, "The cops are coming!"

Danny and I hit the river and started to swim. Rick started the car and took off. The cop went after him. Danny and I made it to the other side of the river. He took off running up the hill, across the road, and down the other side. I wish I had done the same thing, but I thought the cops would be there. Once I got to the other side of the river, I just found the right place to duck down and lie in the leaves. After about a half hour, I heard shouting and gunshots from the other side of the river. I didn't know if Rick was yelling at the cop or the other way around. All I knew was that I was in a bad situation, and I honestly prayed that I would get out of this.

The next thing I knew, I heard cops pull over close by, and then, I heard a dog. Right then, I shit myself. Well, not really, but almost. *Just lie real still.* I was wet, and the weeds were high. They passed within a few feet of me. God must've been with me this time. How could they not see me, or that dog not smell me? They turned back to their car, put the dog in, and drove off. After a few minutes more, another car pulled up, but no one got out. I could hear the police radio and the car running. After about forty-five minutes, it took off—time to make my move.

I stood and ran to the road. I gave a hasty glance left, right, then I ran to the other side, down the hill, and I kept running through wooded areas, backyards, and roads. After about five miles, I felt a little safer, so I would walk, and then run. My mother only lived about ten miles from the river. When I finally made it, I knocked, and she opened it. She asked where I'd been and said Danny had been there for a few hours. "Let me talk to Danny," I said, adding, "I will talk to you later."

She told me he was in the first bedroom, and she went back to bed. I woke him up and asked him if he was okay. He said he was fine and was glad to see me. I let him go back to sleep and cleaned up a little, changed my clothes, took my mother's car, and drove home to watch the news. I didn't have my house keys with me, so I had to knock. Miss T let me in and asked if everything was okay.

I said, "Yes, go back to sleep. I'll join you soon."

I went down to the basement, pulled out my scanner, and turned it on. Then, I turned on the TV. There was nothing about the chase on the TV, but I heard on the scanner that they sent a helicopter to help the police find "three or four men." By now, it was about five hours into this fiasco. They still had not arrested anyone. This was very good for us. After about an hour or so, I put the scanner away. There was no other news, no arrests. I figured Rick had got away, and I started to relax a little, but I still knew this would be all over the news.

An hour later, Rick called. I asked him where he was, and he whispered that he made it back to the cabin. He wanted me to come and get him out of there.

"The cops left over an hour ago," he said.

"Stay where you are, and I'll call you back."

I didn't know what to do. I knew I'd have to ask Miss T for help, and I didn't like that at all. Except, my tools were in the cabin, and if I could get Rick out of there with them, that would be the end of this mess. I knew Rick would never see daylight if the police caught him. He might have even ratted on me if I didn't help him. I made my mind up—*I must go get him*.

I told Miss T I needed her to drive down to where she had dropped me off and that if we were stopped, we'd say we were looking for our friend who had a boat down at the river and come straight back. She did not know what really happened down at the river. She agreed. If she had known what went down, she would not have participated in this adventure.

I called Rick back and instructed him to have the tools and himself ready, I was coming, and, "Be on the lookout."

115

We got in her car, and about twenty minutes later, we were making the right turn on the road to the boat works. I couldn't believe I was going back. I could even hear the helicopter; it was *way* north. Miss T didn't know about the aircraft out searching for us. I didn't know if she even heard it.

As we drove closer to the cabin, it looked good. I told her to pull up to the front door, and Rick came out, carrying some tools. I opened the trunk and said, "Get in the trunk." He jumped right in the trunk, tools and all. It was only one bag, so I ran in, collected the rest, and Miss T drove off.

We made it back to my home. I wanted her to park out back and then go in the house. She did. I let Rick out and told him to go in. Then, I drove over to the stash house. I put all the tools in there and drove back to my home.

Miss T gave Rick some of my clothes. He was all cleaned up, and his girlfriend was coming to get him. We didn't talk too much, and they got out of there as fast as they could.

Everything went back to normal for a few months. I was still working for General Batteries, but Rick and Duke called all the time. I made it clear to them I was not going to do any night work until Big G got out of jail. He had about one year to do yet. Big G would still write to me every few weeks, and I would always send some money.

THE MCDONALD'S JOB

Rick and Duke were out moving around, doing things. They would not work with anyone but Big G or me. Still, Little Joe and

I were out one night doing something, and we made out fair, but little did we know Rick and Duke were down in the same area, doing a McDonald's, and they were not as fortunate as we were. They got busted inside the restaurant. Rick didn't make bail, but Duke did. For the rest of Duke's life, we called him the Hamburglar.

He got seven and a half years for that bust—a lot of time for a crime like that, I thought. He did his time and got out. I have no idea what happened to Rick, but I would still have a few drinks with Duke now and then.

THE COP CHASE

Mike, a big-time pot dealer in Reading whom I'd known for a long time, came out with Danny, me, and this other guy named Bob. We all went up to Kutztown to party. Danny and I drove together, and Mike and Bob rode up together. We found a nightclub that we liked, and it was packed. We were all trying to get laid, but we were too drunk. It was around 12:30 a.m. I stumbled over to Mike and said, "Let's go."

As we bid our farewells, Mike said, "Let's race back to the Chef's Lounge."

I said, "Loser buys drinks the rest of the night."

"You got a deal."

"I'll ride with the winner, and that's gonna be Mike," Danny said.

I knew he was just fucking with me. I put Bob in my Chevy Impala, and Mike and Danny ran over to Mike's Buick. They had a good start on me, about half a mile. We were driving down Route 222, going 100-plus, for fifteen straight minutes. We were moving!

Mike only had a three-block lead now. Then, out of nowhere, this cop pulled out. I knew if Mike pulled over, that cop was going to put him in jail. He also had about a half pound of weed on him. Mike started to slow down, and the police followed suit. Like an asshole, I sped up and passed the cop. The cop pulled around Mike and started coming after me.

Bob was down under the dash. He was praying and asking me to stop. I said to shut the fuck up.

I made it down to Temple, and this was my area. This cop was from Kutztown, or parts around there, and wouldn't know his way around like I did. We came up to a left turn that had a three-way split. He was a few blocks behind. I came to the turn and made a hard left. My back end was sliding. I almost lost it and held on for dear life. So did Bob. We made it around the turn, and I knew he wouldn't see the split until he blew by it, and when he did, he wouldn't know which way I went. I killed my lights and scanned my rearview mirror. Then, he did exactly what I expected—drove straight past, and that was the end of the cop chase.

Next, I found this house that didn't have a car in the driveway, quickly backed in, and turned the car off. I sunk onto the floor with Bob and told him not to say anything. We could hear engines and see headlights now and then. It had to have been the cop. We lay there for about forty minutes, and then, I climbed back into the front seat, told Bob, "If we get stopped, tell them we were at the Temple Bar and Grill." I started the car, and off we drove.

I took the back roads, and we made it to the Chef's Lounge, where we saw Mike's car. When we pulled in, Mike and Danny appeared shocked that we were not in jail. The look on everyone's faces…the two of them must've told the story to everyone already.

Mike paid for everything and anything I wanted, all night long. We all had one hell of a night, but I look back and thank God that no one was hurt or went to jail that night. That was the dumbest thing I'd done in ages, but there's also another lesson in it: always run the other way when you see a cop.

THE END OF MISS T AND ME

Well, with all good things, there comes an end. Miss T and I were no different. I was on the road on the weekends, I worked a full-time job, and I had to keep what I did on the weekends to myself. She always wondered if I was true to her. For the most part, I was, but I came home unexpectedly one weekend, and she wasn't there after telling me she would be. I sensed this scene wasn't right, so I moved my car around the corner, got a beer, and waited till about 2:00 a.m., when she came home.

She sashayed in, and I could tell once she saw me that she'd been out getting laid. She knew I could tell and started to cry. I had an anger problem back then, and I got my gun and made her take me to the man's house, but when I knocked and she asked him to open the door, he threatened to call the cops if I didn't leave. What could I do?

We went back home, and I was not too friendly to her.

Then I got in my car and drove to a friend's home. I went to work the next day, and around lunchtime, the cops came to pick me up because of the guy from last night. They put a bunch of bullshit charges on me, and I was on parole, remember, so this was not good.

It was back to Berks County Jail with another week in quarantine before you could talk to anyone. They gave me a $20,000 cash bail, but I had a parole detainer, so if I had put up the twenty grand, I still wouldn't have gotten out.

Now Miss T had me where she wanted me. She was very much in love with me and would try anything to win me back. What she did not know was if I can't trust you, there's no way I could be around you. It was over. I was not going to stop living my life and doing what I liked to do, not for her. You must remember that you have one life to live—live it the way you want or live to regret it.

Miss T put me through hell for the next three weeks. Then, she started to come around. We wrote to each other and talked on the phone. I told her not to come to the court hearing.

After three times of going to court and her not showing up, the state dropped the charges against me. I guessed they were pissed off. Now, I had to wait and see what the parole board would do. At least I knew a lot of people in this jail, and we could get anything we needed. Everything was going as well as it could.

Miss T and I were writing to each other a lot. I would have her call me once a week and pretend to be my attorney's secretary. The guards would fall for it. I could sit there in the attorney room and talk plainly, knowing they would not be listening to my calls. This worked for over a month, and then someone at the jail called my attorney and asked if he had called me in the past few weeks. He told them the truth because he knew my background and didn't want to get caught up in any bullshit.

The warden summoned me to his office and asked who was calling and pretending to be my attorney. I said, "I can't say, but it was a 'love call,' not any kind of monkey business." He put me in the hole for a week or two. That's a cell under the jail and not a nice place to be.

As the guard was taking me there from the warden's office, he told me that a few of the guards felt like I was using them, and now the rules were going to change. They didn't like change.

The warden made a new policy about inmates getting phone calls from their attorneys. The guards had to call each attorney to verify they needed to speak with their client. I didn't get any more phone calls from mine, but the attorney received a letter from the parole board saying my hearing was six weeks away. I knew that once you beat your case, the board had to let you go.

Six weeks felt like six months, but the day to see the parole board finally came. The hearing was brief. I told them the case against me was dropped because the plaintiff didn't show up at any of court hearings. My parole man was at the hearing, and he announced to the board he thought I was guilty of some of the charges, if not all. The board said they'd let me know what their recommendation was after a talk with my parole officer and put me in a room next door to wait.

After half an hour, my parole man came into the room and informed me he would fight to keep me in on a parole violation, and that he would get his way. He also brought up that he heard I was "into a lot of things" and hoped this would "straighten me out." I knew, right then and there, that I was going to get a violation, but I knew they could not take my street time, so that meant I would do fifteen months, max. That also meant that I was going to the state pen.

Well, the letter came from the parole board, and it was not superb. They did not take my good time, but I had to do the rest of fifteen months, and, about a week later, I was on my way to Graterford State Correctional Institute—the worst prison in Pennsylvania. They had five hundred lifers.

They put me in quarantine when I arrived. All inmates go through this, so they can process you through the system and determine which jail you belong in. I expressed that I wanted to stay in Graterford because I knew I could get a few visits there. They put me in C-Block. Duke was in the same block for the McDonald's stunt he pulled with Rick. I didn't hang out with him. I was doing my own thing.

I took a job as a plumber. Being a plumber in jail gave you access to the whole place. If you needed to see someone on a block or move something between blocks, you could. One time, I tied an ounce of weed inside a mop and put it in the mop bucket. I knew the guard would not pick up the mop because he saw me cleaning up shit water from a cell. A plumber can also make wine from fruit or potatoes and hide it in the pipes throughout the jail.

Time was going as best as it could. Miss T even came to see me and gave me a hundred-dollar bill. I put it under my top lip, and when they checked my mouth, I would keep my lip against my front gums so they couldn't see anything. She would visit every two weeks for about six months. Then, I told her it was over and not to write to me or visit me. I didn't want to waste her time or mine. Time is too precious to waste.

I must say, when you're in jail, you have time to contemplate life, health, and God. I had time to read the Bible, and I tried to make sense of life. My conclusion was: happiness and peace at all costs.

A year ended, and I got to know this one inmate that knew a guard, and this guard would bring in the weed. I wrote a letter to Big G and spelled out how I wanted him to meet with a friend. He instructed me to give this friend the password and his number. The password we used was "money."

I received a letter from Big G telling me that he took care of "the thing" for me a few days ago. Well, now it was time to sit back and hope that all things turned out well. A few days passed by before I got the word that I would be receiving a gift.

After nighttime lockdown, about 10:00 p.m., a guard came by my cell, said, "Here," and speedily dropped off a brown bag. I climbed out of my bunk, picked up the bag, peered in, and it was Christmas. There were about one and a half ounces. The weed had one hell of an aroma. I knew I couldn't light one up in the cell. I had to get this to the stash area. I didn't sleep much that night and got out of my cell as soon as I could.

I put the weed down my pants and headed to the plumbing shop. I rolled up about twenty joints, grabbed my tools, and walked to the bottom of the jail to find an adequate place to smoke one. Once I lit up, it was like heaven.

After about an hour, I got my shit together and drifted up to see some of my friends. I sold about fifteen joints and made five dollars each. That gave me $75 cash. I met with my boys, and we walked casually out to the yard to smoke some more.

Days were going well. I had about four and a half months to go before my time was up. The parole board sent me a letter stating that I would have to see them in two weeks. When they finally called me, they asked if I wanted to go to a halfway house. I told them that they weren't going to tell me what to do, and I then said, "Give the halfway house to someone else."

I stood up and walked out of the room. The guard took me back to my block. My boys asked me what the parole people wanted. I relayed the spiel that they tried to put me in a halfway house, and that I told them no thanks. I would max out.

For real, the last two weeks of my time crept so slow. I thought my release date would never come, but in the end, it did. They called my name and said, "Junk and bunk," which meant, "Get your things and clear your bunk." My mother had sent me some clothing a few weeks prior for this day.

They processed me out, opened the door, and out I went. Big G was there with a new Cadillac. I got in, and off we went.

He had some weed, some beer, and he gave me five hundred bucks. He said, "We have a lot of good things on the books."

We drove to Reading, stopped around, saw some friends, and got drunk. I went to his apartment. He called over a lady friend, and she was with me the rest of the night. The next day, he told me to get an apartment and see my mother. He'd come back for me in a few days.

I rented a furnished apartment on Ninth and Walnut, then left for my mother's. I gave Danny a call, and Zeb, too. We all got together and partied. After about a week of that, it was time to make a plan for my future.

BECOMING A LOCKSMITH

The next thing I did was send off for the Foley Belsaw locksmith home schooling program. I knew that if I were to get locked up again, I could get out if I wanted to. I also knew that this could help me out in other ways. About a week later, I received my books. Then, I bought a key-making machine.

This program taught me how to pick locks, how to open up cars, and how to make keys. The year was around 1978 or 1979. I realize I could've made a decent living out of being a locksmith back then. No license required, which was good for an ex-offender like me. But you know me—I like to do things out of the norm.

THE ACME SUPERMARKET

It was about three weeks until I decided it was time to go and make money. Big G and I headed upstate to look at a few jobs. We were driving around in an old police car Big G had recently acquired. He owned a van now, too. We would use both to do our work.

There was this Acme, and it looked great for a cigarette score. We clocked about one thousand cartons inside. We knew that we could get roughly six dollars a carton from our boys in Allentown or Reading. We both agreed on this score. That was on Saturday, and we did cigarette scores on Wednesday, so it was time to go back to Reading.

I told Big G that I would call Danny B. He said that was cool.

In Reading, Big G went his way, and I went mine. I try to keep heat off me, and being fresh out of jail, I didn't know how much heat Big G had on him. I was always going out of the way to make sure we were not seen together too much. That habit kept the heat off me for years.

I gave Danny a call around 9:00 p.m. that night and asked him to come to my apartment. Once he got there, I explained what Big G and I had and asked him if he was in. He didn't work with us much, but I'd known him for a long time. He told me that he would be proud to work with me and Big G.

Before I knew it, Wednesday had arrived. I received a call from Big G near 10:00 a.m. He told me to call Danny, and to be ready at about 10:00 p.m. He wanted to meet him at Ninth Street, near the bar. I was there at 10:00 p.m., and Big G was there about the same time. He picked me up in his car and gave me the keys to the van. We turned down Eleventh Street to pick it up. He dropped me off about a block away and confirmed where to meet him. I hustled to the van, got in, and drove off to get him on Twelfth Street. Then, we went to get Danny on the other side of town.

Danny was ready, so off we went to the Acme, which was only two hours away, so we were not going to need a room. We had walkie-talkies and a scanner set up for the state police and the local police. I told Danny to park the van before finding a quality lookout spot and then give us the green light.

This was my first job since getting out of jail. We would only be carrying a light in-tool bag. We would not need to take a torch bag with us, since we were going in for nothing but the smokes and some shopping. Once we reached the score, we cruised by to check it out—wonderful. Then, we searched for some parking and an acceptable drop-off area. We found what we were looking for—a little far away, but still good parking—and we stopped the van so Danny could get in the driver seat. I climbed in the back, dug out the walkie-talkies and scanner, and turned them on. Everything was working well, so Danny took us to the drop-off area and let us out.

Big G and I made our way out back of the supermarket, and everything still looked good. We knew that it would take Danny about twenty minutes to park and get into position. We had the scanner and one walkie-talkie. Danny gave us a call with the green light, and we made our way to the back door. If that didn't work, there was a vent near the top of the roof that we could get in.

I picked two large screwdrivers out of the bag, stuck them in near the top deadbolt, and gave it just a little pressure. The door popped open. Big G came over once he saw the door pop and radioed Danny to be on his toes. Danny said, "We still have a green light." So, in we went, straight to the office to shake it down and make sure there was not an alarm system we overlooked. Big G gave the all clear. We tried the safe, just to see if it was on day lock. We were not that lucky. I made for the back to find boxes for the cigarettes. We used egg boxes; they were spacious and would hold plenty of cartons. I also found a four-wheeled cart. I put the egg boxes on that, and a few feet down to the right, I saw what looked like cigarette cartons, and—lord behold—there were about five hundred more cartons of cigarettes in boxes.

I wheeled the cart to the front, got another green light from Danny, and started to put the cigarettes on it. As we were doing that, I was telling Big G what I'd found in the back. He said, "We'll get them on our way out," and by the time we left, we estimated about 1,500–2,000 cartons. We would get six to seven dollars each, so that gave us $9,000–$12,000, and we were only in the store for about an hour and a half. Now, it was time to go shopping.

We took all the gloves, all the batteries, all the top steaks, and anything else we could use. We carried everything to the back door and asked Danny for a green light. Everything was green. Big G and I ran out back to the tree line. I gave Danny a call and said, "I'll come around and take your place, so you can go get the van." Everything was quiet—nothing on the police scanner, no cars coming by. It was perfect.

I crept to where Danny was. I said, "Go get the van." I had one walkie-talkie. He had the other. When he came down the road, Danny flashed the headlights. I gave him the green light, and he drove around back. It took about twenty minutes. I received a call from Danny, who said they were coming to get me. I gave them a green light and saw the lights coming up alongside the store. I started to walk and gave them the flashlight sign. They saw me, picked me up, and off we went. In truth, the feeling I got when I did a score is something I still miss.

We made it back to the stash area. Danny and I took a few cartons each. Big G and I would make a few calls to the friends who handled hot things.

Three days later, Pete from Allentown took them all. We drew around $12,500 in cash for the whole thing. Danny, Big G, and I got together and had a little party. When we were partying, I reminded Big G not to forget that we could go back and do it all over again. The vent that I'd seen would be easy to get in. He said, "That's a good thing to remember."

We partied at Chef's Lounge bar at 9th Street in Reading. That was our bar. I didn't have a steady girl. I strictly dated. I didn't want any problems in my life.

When it was time to go, I walked around and said my goodbyes. There were about twenty people at the party, but I went home by myself.

That night, I met this new guy that Big G knew named Gary. He used to run with Big G, and I knew he'd be a part of our crew eventually. I was trying to adjust to this way of life again. I knew that I'd be going back to jail if I kept it up, but I decided that this was what I was meant to do. As my life progressed, it was harder to accept. I had many good jobs that most people would've loved, but nothing brought me more happiness than doing night jobs with my crew.

Little Joe gave me a call to say hello and to see if I was doing nighttime work yet. I vented about how I had decided to do *only* night work. No daytime work anymore, unless I owned the business. He told me he would call me in a few weeks, and that was cool with me.

THE JACK DANIEL'S SAFE

I received a call from Big G, who told me that Gary wanted us to come to Delaware and behold this safe job he found. It was Wednesday, and we would go down on Friday. I said, "I'm in." He told me to come to his house about 9:00 a.m. and pack a bag, and I said, "I'll be there."

9:00 a.m. sharp, we got in Big G's car, and he told me we were going to Milton, Delaware, and that Gary had a house down there. About three hours later, we pulled into Gary's. He came out to greet us and handed us a couple of beers. We sat around and drank a few cold ones. After about twenty minutes, I asked him about the safe. He said, "It's black, with big wheels that are about three inches in diameter." It sounded like an antique one to me.

I asked him where this score was, and he told me Middletown, Delaware. That was about two hours northwest from where we were. I was in a hurry to see this old safe. I asked Gary to get his overnight bag together, but he suggested we could all come back to his place and sleep since no one else was there. With that, we hopped in the car and took off.

Two and a half hours later, we were at the score—a liquor store. Big G wanted me to go in while it was still open for business and look around. I asked Gary where the safe was. He said, "Behind the counter to the right." I had been on the road, off and on, for about five hours, and now it was time to go to work. I got out of the car and walked into the liquor store, staying away from the counter, so I didn't look suspicious. I picked out a bottle of wine and made my way over to the counter. There were three people in front of me, which gave me a chance to dawdle over to where the safe was, and, lo and behold, there it was. It was black with three-inch wheels alright, with the name Jack Daniel's written across the front. Now, I want to remind you readers, this was the first time I did anything with Gary.

It was made of cardboard. An advertisement! I started to laugh, knowing Big G would get a laugh out of this. I decided that I would make him come in and look. I paid for my wine and returned to the car. I described to Big G that it was a pretty old safe and we could open it in a second, but he'd better check it out, too. He stepped out of the car and went inside.

About three minutes later, he came out and flashed a look at me. I was in the driver's seat, sporting an enormous grin. He got in and asked Gary to go in, saying he couldn't quite make out the name on the safe. Once Gary was gone, Big G asked me if I thought Gary was not right in some way. I put it to Big G that Gary was *his* boy, and I laughed. He told me to go fuck myself.

Gary came out, got in the car, and clarified, "The safe said Jack Daniel's, and that was the only safe I saw." I had to break the news to Gary that the safe was made out of cardboard. He could not comprehend what I was telling him. Big G told me to drive around Middletown for reconnaissance.

We found a supermarket that we liked, drove back to Route 113 South, and were on our way back to Milton when we stopped to eat at this restaurant inside an old ship. They had great food, and we sat near the office. As we were eating, the manager stepped into the office. We couldn't help but notice he'd left the door open.

131

Big G and I saw two modest safes inside that I knew we could open in about twenty minutes. Big G and I could not believe what we were seeing. Gary unaffectedly kept eating and did not see anything. Big G and I did not say anything.

We paid for our food and left. On our way back to Gary's, we saw a VFW we liked. We put it on the list.

The next day, Big G and I woke up, packed up the car, and drove into Lewes, Delaware. We drove onto the Cape May-Lewes Ferry. They had food and drinks, so we ordered breakfast for the hour-long ride. It was a great time relaxing on a beautiful day.

We drove off the ferry in New Jersey and headed back to Reading. It was Saturday night, and I went home. I told Big G I wanted to do the restaurant and the VFW. He told me he would call me.

THE FERRY JOB

A few weeks went by, and Gary gave me a call. It was two weeks before Labor Day. He asked me to come down and get a load of something he'd found. I asked him if it was cardboard safe, and we both had a laugh. He said, "This is a first-class score, with a real safe and big money."

I said, "I'll be down in a few days." That was on a Wednesday.

Saturday, around 10:00 a.m., I headed down to Milton. A few hours later, I gave Gary a call, told him I was around the corner from his house, and said to get ready. He told me he was ready. I pulled up, and he told me we'd take his car. It had Delaware plates.

I had Pennsylvania plates on my van, and if we were going to drive around and look at scores, it would be better. As we headed to Lewes, I asked him what we were going to see.

He said, "I have a bank, an Eagles Club, and we are going to mark the Cape May-Lewes Ferry on the Delaware Bay."

"Sounds like we're going to have a busy day," I said.

About an hour later, he pulled into the bank. It was superb. It was away from people's homes, and it had parking for my men. It wasn't open, so I asked him to pull into the parking lot and kill the engine. I wanted to see if they had teller safes. I made a beeline to the outside teller window and peeped in real quick. I saw four safes behind the main counter where the tellers worked. I got back to the car and told Gary to get us out of there. He started to drive, and then he asked me how it looked.

I told him it was going on the list. "We should do this job next." He headed over to the Eagles Club that he had found. I always made money out of these clubs. This one had a few cars in it, and it didn't have an alarm system. I told him to park near the dumpster while I took a quick look. No one was around, so I got out and peeked in the dumpster. They had punchboards, which meant they had gambling.

I got back in the car and said to Gary, "This is a good club, we'll put this on the list. You know what, Gary? I'm impressed. Last time you took me to show me a score it was cardboard." He told me to go fuck myself.

Saving the best for last, according to Gary, we made our way over to the other side of town, toward the Lewes Ferry Terminal. He pulled over to a parking lot, away from the main one. He pointed out that inside the building where the cars stopped to pay their fare was a square-door safe. The building was detached from the main structure, accessible, and I saw a lot of cars lined up to pay for a ride on the ferry—and Labor Day weekend was just around the corner.

I spelled it out for Gary and said I wanted to come back on Sunday night and rehearse this score, because it was the best out of them all.

We headed back to his house, and I asked what his plans were for the evening. He told me he was going to see his girlfriend. I said, "I'm going to go to Ocean City to get a room. I'll be back Sunday night around 11:00 p.m." We agreed to use his car, not take any tools, and look at that safe.

About two hours later, I was in Ocean City. I love that place. It's authentically beautiful and full of beautiful women. I rented a room, grabbed something to eat, toured the boardwalk, and found a place to sit and watch the ocean—and the women—for a few hours. Afterward, I returned to my room and slept.

The next day, I woke up around 11:00 a.m. and, for the most part, I just hung out. I was on the ocean side, and my room was on the seventh floor. I had my curtains open to the beautiful ocean view. Gradually, 10:00 p.m. rolled around. It was time to head over to Gary's house. I put some dark clothing on, got in my car, and when I showed up to Gary's house, he was already outside waiting. I pulled out a flashlight and a pair of gloves. We got in Gary's car and started to drive.

The ferry's last run was around 9:00 or 10:00 p.m. It was now after 11:00 p.m. There was a camper and a few cars. I pointed to a spot where I wanted Gary to drop me. Before I got out of the car, I told him to take about an hour ride, and I would give him two flashes with the flashlight when I saw him. Then, I slipped into the woods unseen.

I slowly made my way over to the building where the safe was. I turned my flashlight on and looked in through the window and around the building. I found what I was looking for—a medium-sized safe and no alarm on the building.

It was time to go. I made my way back to the pickup area and found a spot to wait for Gary. There were a few more cars in the parking area, waiting for the morning ferry. I was only there for ten minutes, and then came Gary. I gave him the signal, flashlight off and on two times.

He pulled up, and I got in. "I love that score," I said. I added, "This could bring about twenty to thirty thousand dollars," and that put a big smile on his face. Then, I told him I was going to get Big G.

"We could open that safe in about one hour."

"Cool."

"We should do this job on Labor Day weekend, on Sunday night. Hopefully, the holiday money will be there."

We drove in silence a bit. In two weeks, we would be down to do this job.

"I'll call you on Friday and let you know if it's on or off," I finally said.

We made it back to Gary's, and I put my gloves and flashlight back in my trunk. I had a few beers, rolled up some weed, and we smoked. It was around 3:00 a.m. when I fell asleep.

I woke up around 10:00 a.m. Gary and I rambled about and ate some breakfast before coming back to his home. I got in my car and drove to the ferry. I had to wait an hour before it pulled in.

I paid the man in the booth, took another long look at the score, and drove my car onto the ferry. I exited the vehicle, ordered a beer, and explored to the top deck for a bird's eye view at the score. Strangely, every time I looked, it got better and better.

The ferry pulled out, and about two hours later, I was in Cape May, New Jersey. Then, I drove to Atlantic City, hung out there for a few hours, and then headed home. When I came back to Reading, I gave Big G a call. No answer. I decided to call him in a few days.

It wasn't until the following Thursday that I got in touch with Big G and we met at a bar in Reading. I told him about my trip to Delaware and about the bank and the club I liked. Then, I put across the ferry job to him. He said, "I've been on that boat a few times and never looked at it as a score."

I added, "It is a medium-sized square door. It'll take some time to open."

He said, "I'm in for the job."

"I would like to get a look at the tools next Thursday, to see if we need to pick up anything," I said, adding, "We are going to make some money."

We had some lunch. Afterward, I told him I would pick him up at his home around 10:00 a.m., and I would not call him if everything was a go. He replied the same, and when Thursday came, I went over to Big G's, and he was ready to go. We got in my car drove to the stash house. We put our gloves on and looked through all the tools, and the only thing we needed was some batteries for the scanner and the walkie-talkies.

I told Big G I would pick up the batteries, and we organized the tool kits. Then we put the radio bag, the in-tool bag, and the torch bag near the door, so when we came back, it would not take us much time to put them in the trunk.

Since I'd already seen the score, all Big G had to do was drive by and drive away.

Saturday came. I called Big G around 10:00 a.m., but he didn't pick up the phone. I tried him again at 1:00 p.m. Same thing. I tried again and again and again with no luck. It was Labor Day weekend, so I figured he must've been partying. I only wished he would've called and set it right with me that he was not in on this job.

It was 6:00 p.m., and still no Big G.

I rolled to the stash house and collected all the tools, but didn't take the torch set, which takes two people to work. I would take the radio bag and the Johnson bar (a five-foot bar with a flat end, a round top, and some weight to it).

I walked to a payphone and gave Big G one last call. No answer. I gave Gary a call, said I was on my way, and explained about Big G. He told me he was ready. I hung up the phone and drove. I pulled in to Gary's around 10:00 p.m. He came out to meet me, as usual, and I asked him if anyone was here. He said, "It's just us."

I took the radio bag out and brought it into the house, then fished out the walkie-talkie and scanner. I put new batteries in everything and the Cape May chip in the scanner. We turned the scanner on, but we didn't hear anything—probably too far away. The walkie-talkies worked well. We then had some beers and some burgers and went to bed.

We woke up Sunday around 10:00 a.m. and put the tools in Gary's car. We went out, found something to eat, and went back to Gary's house. We wouldn't have to leave his house until around 11:00 p.m. That would put us there around 12:00 or 12:30 a.m., and we could start work by 1:00 a.m.

We drove back to Gary's home. He showed me around his property. He had about ten acres. After he showed me his land, we walked back to his house and rested.

11:00 p.m. came, and Gary and I got in his car. We set off to the score and drove by. To my surprise, there were not too many cars there in the parking lot. That was useful for us. A few miles away, we parked and removed the tools, the radios, and the Johnson bar from the trunk. I got the scanner out and turned it on. We heard the police talking about an accident in the area. I turned on the radio, still working. I wished Big G had been there with us; it would've made it easier for me, but it was time for Gary to drop me off, so we headed back to the score.

Everything still looked green. Gary pulled over. I got out, took the in-tool bag, the Johnson bar, and the radio with me. I made my way over to where I had gone in a few weeks ago, and nothing had changed. I squeezed in between the tree and the fence, pulling the in-tool bag and the Johnson bar in with me. I made my way to the office where the safe was. I picked two screwdrivers out and popped the door open—it was easy, and I didn't make any noise. I asked Gary for a green light, and he gave me one. I used a hammer to knock the dial off the safe. I then got a punch out and tried to punch the safe. That didn't work.

I asked Gary for a green light. He gave me the green light. I asked him about the noise, and he said, "Green." This damn safe was not opening! I would have to peel the door open, so I took a chisel out, put it in the crack of the door, and started to hammer.

The corner bent. I grabbed the Johnson bar, put it in the bent corner, and began to pry the front door open. This was an unquestionably heavy-duty lockbox. A few hours elapsed, and I only had it halfway open. It was going slow.

Then, I got lucky. I pushed down again, and it opened three-fourths of the way, to the point where I could reach to the cement that covered the locking bolts. I hammered the cement away enough to see the hardened bolts. I fit the Johnson bar behind them and pried them out of the holes. The safe came open.

I started to put the money in the in-tool bag when three cars pulled in. I turned on the radio and asked for a green light. Gary called me back with a green light. He figured they were just tourists parking for the ferry. I went back to work, finished putting the money in the bag, and then I called Gary for a green light. He called me back with a one. I asked him to get ready for the pickup. I left the office with everything I had brought with me and more.

Gary pulled in as I reached the pickup area. He popped the trunk, I threw everything in, and off we went. We got out of there at the right time. It was the beginning of dawn.

We made it back to Gary's house and pulled the in-tool bag out of the trunk as we rushed into his house. We counted up the money, and it came to about fifteen thousand dollars. We decided to give Big G 10 percent of the take. I was tickled that it turned out the way it did. I slept until 1:00 p.m. the next day, cleaned up all the tools, and walked out to get the paper. There it was on the front page: *Thieves get away with thousands of dollars from the safe at the Lewes Terminal.*

I told Gary that I would stay one more day, and he said, "You can stay as long as you want." Gary and I went out all over his town. We had some crabs, clams, and other seafood. We hit the one bar he frequented and had a few drinks. Then I said, "It's time to go back to your home. I don't want too many people to see us together." We drove back to Gary's and laid around for the rest of the day.

I woke up around 9:00 a.m. I woke Gary and said, "I'm going home now, and think I'll take the ferry back to New Jersey." He looked at me like I was completely nuts.

We said our goodbyes, and off I went.

It was Tuesday, two days after the fact. I pulled up to the terminal, and the ferry was loading. When I paid my fare and drove on, I looked over and saw an alarm box on the office. That didn't surprise me. Here I was with the tools in my trunk and my part of the money in my pocket. I parked my car, walked to the bar, and grabbed a beer.

The ferry left Lewes, and I was reflecting on the night we did the score. Then, someone called out my name, and I almost shit my pants. It was some guy that had worked on my cars a few times before. He had also worked for the mob as an arsonist. He and some girl sat down, and he asked what I was doing down here. I told him I was down in Ocean City seeing some girl. He said that was cool and that his family had a house in Lewes. I said, "That's cool." We talked about bullshit for about an hour. I said goodbye and went back for one more beer.

I took that he knew what I was doing there, but he didn't say anything. I sipped my beer, and about ten minutes later, the ferry was pulling in to the dock. I made my way down to my car, drove off the boat, and pushed back to Reading.

I stopped and called Big G. This time, he picked up. I told him that I was going to stop over, and he said, "Okay."

Big G opened his door before I could knock. I asked him where the hell he'd been. He went into detail about how he was with some honey. I said, "You missed out on some good money."

He told me, "We can always make money, but we can't always get good pussy."

He asked me how it went. I told him what happened, and that I had a few dollars for him. That made him happy. Big G could act strange sometimes, but I still looked up to him and liked staying on his good side. I think he needed me. I never asked him too many questions or pried too much into his excuses. He was a friend, and friends take care of one another.

GETTING SHOT AT

Big G called me two weeks later. He told me we were going up around Williamsport and to pack a bag. It was an unusually small town. We guessed the cops would be home by midnight. I told him I had a bag in my car.

He picked me up, and we picked up the old police car, which had all the tools in it. It took us about three hours to get up there. We looked at a drugstore we had on the list, and it was promising. We cruised through a few other towns, and we ran across a jewelry store that we both loved.

Next to the jeweler's was an empty store that was not wired for alarms. The jewelry store only had a bell on the outside with no battery in it, and alarm clips on the doors. Once we got in, we would unscrew the clips from the door that we wanted to use and tape them together. The alarms that had batteries could be filled with caulk so that no one would hear them ring.

We figured we would go in the empty store, go through the wall, do the safe, and go home with the jewelry. We always liked doing jewelry stores on Saturdays, because back in the late '70s, they were not open on Sundays.

We rented a room for about an hour away. We chose not to call anyone to help us. We were excited to do this ourselves. We stepped out for some food, took it back to the room, and pulled out the scanner and the in-tool bag. We always enjoyed listening to the scanner to see what kind of scandals were going on in the area. Back in the old days, we would have to go out and find the frequency crystal for that area and put it in the scanner. But now, we just had to open a frequency book, look up the town, and punch the right frequency in.

Everything was quiet on the scanner, and that was comforting. I put new batteries in the walkie-talkies, wiped off all the in-tools, and it was time to take it easy until midnight.

About one hour later, we were driving by the score, and everything was just right for the job. Big G dropped me off with the in-tool bag. He parked the car and walked over to the drop-off area. We took a few tools out, went to the empty store, and precisely when we swung the door open, a cop car came out of nowhere.

Big G and I were off to the races. We ran down the block. The cop jumped out of his car and yelled, "Stop, or I'll shoot your face off!" He fired his gun at us. Bullets were flying all around.

We made it to the end of the block, around to the back stores, and down over the hill. We stopped for a minute and checked each other. "Did you get shot?"

We both said, "No." We had to stay calm and get out of this town. I started to think, *If they pick us up, what could they get us for? Breaking into an empty building?* The only evidence was the in-tool bag because they didn't get the torch set. That was good. They could only get us for attempted burglary, and that was okay.

We started making our way to where we had parked the car. We didn't see any cops around. We could see our car, but we decided to wait until people started to go to work so we could blend in. So we watched the car for about three hours before we made our move. Big G sat in the driver's seat. I sank way down in the passenger seat so that no one could see me. We took off. As luck had it, we didn't see any police. We were out of that town and on our way back to Reading.

After a few hours of driving, we were back in Reading. We put the car away and said our goodbyes. Big G told me he would be in touch. Out of all the delinquent things I'd done, that was the only time I'd ever been shot at. We never returned to that town.

EERIE AROUND ERIE

Big G gave me a call, and he wanted to go up around Erie. "I'm in," I said. I always made money in western Pennsylvania. It was Tuesday, and he wanted to see me on Thursday around 1:00 p.m. at his apartment.

He saw me pulling in, right on time, and opened the door.

"Are you ready to make money?" he asked.

"Always."

He pulled the Pennsylvania map out, and we examined it. We decided to start at Meadville. For that, we would take two cars. We would also bring Danny and this guy, Bob, who was married and would come out every six months or so, hoping to make a few thousand. Big G had known him for a long time, and I had worked with him a few times.

Danny and I decided we would ride in the van, and Big G and Bob would ride in the old police car. We were to leave on Friday around 9:00 a.m., so we all met at the stash house where we kept the cop car and put our personal items in the trunk, on top of the tools. Big G and Bob got in that car, while Danny and I drove my car over to where the van was stashed. We would meet them on the Pennsylvania Turnpike, up around Harrisburg.

We had CB radios in each vehicle and used Channel 32 most of the time to stay in touch. We bought gas at a rest area and headed back on the road.

We reached Meadville around 3:00 p.m. We parked the van and drove around town. We didn't see much we liked, so we moved on. Danny and I headed north in the van to Saegertown. Around here, we found a drugstore we liked, but we did those scores on Wednesdays, and it was a Friday.

North we went, and the next stop would be Edinburg. We saw an Eagles Club we liked. "Let's get a room and get a good night's sleep and look again tomorrow," Big G suggested, and we rented two adjoining rooms under fake names.

After dinner, we cruised by the Eagles Club to see how the business was. It was inviting. We went back to the room, talked a little, and sacked out. We woke up around 10:00 a.m., put our gear in the car, went out for breakfast, and used that time to scan the map again. Big G wanted to go up to Waterford. I wanted to go to Albion. So, we decided to split up.

Well, Danny and I didn't see too much there, so we drove back to Route 18 and then north. There were a few towns, but we didn't see anything we liked. We headed toward Franklin Center. Then, after that, Danny and I were on this back road and saw a path going down into the woods. I decided to stop, take a piss, and smoke a joint.

There were no homes or anything around. I pulled over and told Danny to roll one. He brought out one he had already rolled, so we got out of the car and hiked down this path about a quarter of a mile, and I lit the joint. We walked into this opening, and I jumped out of my skin. We stepped into this clearing, and there was a marble pad, about eight feet wide by twenty feet long. It had three benches on each side, and at the end of the marble pad, there was an altar. It was three feet high and eight feet long. On top of the platform was a cow statue. There was a concave crevice where the cow's stomach would be, and it looked like people had been setting something in it. Danny was behind me. I warned him to be on his toes.

I fucking could not believe my eyes. I walked up to the idol and just stared at it. There was a little path going farther into the woods. I told Danny to go look down that path.

I sat down and smoked some more weed as Danny looked around.

He was scared and wanted to get out of there. I sent him to go look out on the road and let me know if anything was going on. Meanwhile, I sat there, gave the place a good look around, and smoked my weed.

Danny yelled, "Come on. I want to go."

I took one last look around and walked out of the woods. Danny was at the car, and you could tell he wanted to get the hell out of there. Me? I didn't want the people who put this altar thing together to see us there, because we didn't know what they were up to. This was around the time farmers were finding cows in the fields all cut up.

It was time to go. We got in the car and drove off.

Danny and I met up with Big G and Bob up in Erie. We shared with them our story, and they just looked at us as if we were nuts. I guess you had to be there. Anyway, it was time to get a room. Once we had our room and put everything away, we went out for dinner and talked about things. The next day, we would head south over to Union City and go from there.

Bob and Big G crashed early. Danny and I wanted to go out to a club. The clubs in Erie were a lot of fun, and we were not going to work in Erie, so it wasn't a risk, but Danny and I could not get what we'd seen off our minds. We wonder to this day what it was.

We woke up the next day, and we all headed over to Union City. We saw a few good clubs and put one we liked on the list. We rented a room around Oil City. I liked a few things in Oil City, but that's another story. After checking in, we brought all the tools in and inspected them. Everything was ready to go. It was Saturday. We had time to rest. I went out for some beer, but other than that, we stayed in our rooms, naturally.

Around 11:00 p.m., it was time to go. When we put the tools into the car, we made sure no one saw us. Big G and Bob got into the van. Danny and I got into the car. We were about one and a half hours from the score. We finally arrived and found parking for the van. Danny and I got into the car. Bob was the designated driver for tonight, and we drove by the score. Everything seemed shipshape. Bob stopped the car and popped the trunk, and we pulled the tools out.

We pulled the CB radios out and checked with Bob.

"Green light."

We put Danny in a lookout position out front, and Big G and I went around to the back door. We were in there in no time. Big G checked the office, and I looked for the bar. I opened a door, and to my surprise, there were fifteen slot machines. I took two screwdrivers and started to pop open the doors at the bottom of the slots. They were full. I was amazed that all these slot machines were in this club. This was all illegal money. Big G came around the corner, and he could not believe what he was seeing.

He told me there was no safe, but we found three mop buckets and started to put the quarters in them. We filled them, and we put the rest of the quarters in the boxes that were in the slots. It was a lot of quarters, but it didn't take us long. I'm guessing we were in the hot zone for about twenty minutes.

We called Bob to come around to the pickup area.

"I'll be there in ten minutes."

We called Danny for a green light, and we got one. We took the tools and two of the mop buckets out to where Danny was and hurried back for the other bucket and boxes. By the time we trudged back with the last of it, Bob was there at the pickup. We put everything in the trunk and off we went. Once we were out of there, Big G and I started to talk about what we'd seen. We had been doing scores for a little while, and we had never seen that many slot machines.

We picked up the van and headed to the room. We brought the money inside and left the tools in the car. I found a large cup, filled it with quarters, and started making four piles. We would not bother counting them out. We each took our share of the money. Then, we put it in the van—always keep the money and the tools separate. We cleaned up the room and headed back to Reading, a six-hour drive.

Once back in Reading, we parked the car and van back at the stash place. We all took our money and went our separate ways. Me, I got my car and headed down to Atlantic City. I finished at Caesars Casino and found that taking quarters into casinos and cashing them in was no problem. Back then, no one even looked at you funny. I cashed in and had about $1,900. That was a good night.

I rented a room, gave Big G a call, and he told me he was coming down tomorrow. We had a ball down there. We went back to Reading, and he told me he would call.

TIME, AND LIFE, MOVES ON

Big G called me when it was time to do jobs in Delaware. Since the ferry job, Gary and I had become great friends. We went back and did the supermarket again.

My crew did things all over New York, Maryland, New Jersey, Delaware, and Connecticut. We moved around a lot over the next few years, hitting supermarkets, clubs, drugstores, jewelry stores. It started to feel like the same old thing, week after week. We made a lot of money without any problems. But after a while, I was looking for something new. I wanted to do some heavier things, so I set out looking at banks and found one.

D&G VITAMINS STORES

Big G, Danny, and I moved to New Jersey. We rented a three-bedroom house in Barnegat, and I met a girl who lived down there named Christine. She was eighteen years old, and I was in my late twenties. We would go out and do our thing, and she would look after our place.

One weekend, when we were not doing anything, Danny asked me if I would go down to Barrington, New Jersey. He was trying to find this one vitamin store that sold stimulants and sleep aids. He bought some black beauties, fun little speed pills. The stimulants were caffeine and ephedrine, and back in the day, it was legal to have the two together. They had robin eggs, the tablets that looked like speed. They had sleep aids that looked like Quaaludes, yellows, and Tuinal blue tips. My jaw dropped at what I was seeing.

We got into the car and took two each, and they were exactly like taking the real thing. By the time we got back to Barnegat, we were speeding our asses off.

The next day, I drove back down to the vitamin store and bought six-thousand-pill jars of black beauties for six hundred dollars. When I got back to Barnegat, I called all my boys all excited about the six thousand black beauties I had for sale. A few days carried on, and I had sold all the pills and made six thousand. Then, after a few days, I got calls for more.

The vitamin store left the wholesaler's address on the bottle. The distributor was out of Lewisburg. I got them on the phone, and they spelled out what they needed from me—a store license, a federal tax license—before I could buy any pills directly from them.

I went to Gary and said that I wanted to open a store. He didn't have any money, so he went and borrowed four thousand from a friend of ours named Sal P., a well-known gangster in the area. This loan would help Gary out when the FBI came after us.

The distributor also informed us that we would have to be prepared to purchase 4,000 dollars' worth of pills at a time. I talked to my lawyer and put him on the papers while I looked for a store. I also asked about the legality of breaking down thousand-pill jars into hundred jars, and, as long as I had a sterile place, I would have no problem.

I found a storefront on Tenth Street in Reading, rented it, and we called it D&G Vitamins. I ordered jars with my store's name on them that held a hundred pills. I put a laminated table in the back that I could easily keep sterile. I bought three long, glass counters to put all the stimulant pills and the sleep aids in. I also sold regular vitamins in the store. Our slogan was "Reducing while you maintain energy."

I called with my order for more speed pills and sleep aids. I bought one thousand pills for twenty dollars, sold off one hundred for twenty dollars, and made 180 dollars. I was open seven days a week, but, at first, business was slow.

Gary could not sit in the store for ten hours a day, and after a few months, he wanted out. So, I gave him his money back, and the store was mine. Within a month, I was in another storefront over on Ninth, where they parked hundreds of buses each weekend for the outlet stores on Moss Street. I had Christine hand out flyers with a 10 percent discount on it to all the people that stepped off the buses. Before I knew it, I was making a lot of money selling fake speed pills and fake downers.

The DEA didn't like these pills at all. When they arrested people on the street with these pills, they could not win the cases.

I was happy about my life at that time. We moved back to Reading because I was there more than in my house in New Jersey. Big G, Danny, and I rented a house on Cross Keys Road by all the Burn Township farms—my old stomping grounds—on the outskirts of town. Christine would come up and stay a few weeks and then run along back home. Things were going great for me.

D&G VITAMINS STORE IN NEW BRUNSWICK, NJ

Christine had a brother going to Rutgers University–New Brunswick named Ron. I traveled up there to see her brother, and I loved the area for a D&G Vitamins store, so I found a storefront a few blocks from the university and opened another shop. I started to make money right off the bat. Christine's brother worked for me. The kids loved my store. They kept telling him that they didn't know what they would do without us.

I would go up from Reading to New Brunswick once a week to restock, go over the books, pick up my money, and pay Ron, and he even hired a helper. We sold more stimulants than sleep aids in both my stores. I want to tell you, I sold a lot of vitamins, too.

Sometimes, I would stay over and party with the university girls. Ron didn't know about my night job, and, for the most part, neither did a lot of people. That was okay with me.

• • • • • • • • • • • • •

PART IV

GROWING WEED

It was the beginning of spring, and I decided to try something new. I got together with Big G, Danny, and my pot dealer, Mike, and declared that I wanted to grow weed. I thought for sure Mike knew how to do this. So, the four of us decided that we would try our hand at it.

We scoured Burn Township farms for a cornfield that had a stream flowing around it, so we wouldn't have to haul in water. There were plenty of meandering streams in this area, but we also had to stay as far away from other homes and farms as possible. We were hoping we would get lucky.

Once we were out to Burn Township, we drove around for two hours and turned down this one road with cornfields on both sides. They had barely planted the corn a month ago, and it was coming up. We passed a farmhouse and spotted a meandering stream on the right of the road. We drove alongside it for about two miles. The road made a right turn, and that put us on a path we knew. This was it: a perfect spot to try this new endeavor.

We headed back to Mike's place and discussed what we needed. We all smoked weed and saved the seeds from our first-rate pot. Mike pointed out that we would need dissolving pods. I didn't know what he was even talking about. He explained that it was a soil-based pod you put your seed in and then set on the ground. Then, once the plant came up, you planted the whole pod, and as the seed grew, the pod would dissolve.

I asked, "Why can't we just plant the seed where we want it to grow?"

He explained how the rabbits and squirrels would eat the smaller plants. I then asked him if the rabbits and the squirrels liked to get high. He got a little mad because this was no little thing. He told me he didn't know if they got high, but we would need some fencing to keep them out.

I asked him how many pods we would need, and he said five hundred, which was too many to buy at one place. He had us go around different stores to buy fifty at a time—more than that, and some stores would look at you funny, and we didn't want any heat.

The stage was set, and the meeting was over, so we departed to the bar, had a few beers, and said our goodbyes.

Mike picked up the fencing because he knew what he needed. I made a few phone calls, and one of my friends said he could help, but he wanted to be able to buy some of the weed at a good price. I said, "You got a deal." He agreed to pick up the pods for me and would give me a call in a day or so.

A few days passed, and my friend called me to say he had everything and wanted to meet. I gave him the money I owed him, and as we were loading the pods in the trunk of my car, he told me not to forget him when it was harvest time. I said, "You will be one of the first people I'll call."

We had everything together, and it was time to plant some weed. Big G picked me up. We transferred all the pods from my trunk to his van, and then we went to pick up Mike and Danny. We stopped for gas because we knew this would take some time. We made our way over to Burn Township, toward the cornfield we had picked out. We cruised by the farmhouse, and everything looked well enough, so we decided to make the drop off without going around again.

The pods were in large trash bags. Danny and I grabbed the bags. I told Mike to get everything out of the van. It took us a few minutes to get everything out, and we always wore gloves. We didn't touch anything without gloves.

We dropped the bags at the bottom of the hill and went back for the rest of the supplies, putting everything out of sight from the road. Big G gave me a walkie-talkie, and he had a CB radio in the van. Danny, Mike, and I would go out and work while he drove around until we finished.

One good thing about the site we had selected was that it was well hidden. There was about a four-foot hill you had to go down, then there were a few trees, then a stream that you had to jump across—it was only a few feet wide—and then you were in our cornfield.

I requested a radio check from Big G, and everything was super. Danny, Mike, and I brushed around and found a neat place to set everything up inside a group of trees. There was enough space where we could install the fencing and lay the pods in the middle. The stream was right there, so watering the plants was simple.

We brought our supplies over. In one of the buckets, Mike had a hammer and three pocket knives. He said, "Next time, we bring three shovels." He gave Danny and me knives and handed Danny a bucket. He and Danny fetched water.

Mike then demonstrated how one man would wet the pods, and two men would poke a little hole in the center of each pod, about halfway down, stick about three to five seeds in each, seal the top, set the pod down, and repeat until we had all the pods done.

I gave Big G a call on the radio and ordered him to take off for about three hours. He called back and told us we had a green light, and he would give us a call in a few hours. We all reached into our pockets and pulled out our seeds.

After seeding, we moved the pods to where they could flourish. Then, we braced the fence poles, hammered them into the ground, and hooked the fence to the poles. We wrapped the fence around the area two times. The last thing we did was put our gloves in the buckets and hide the buckets.

It was about four weeks until I had time to get with Mike and check the plants. I called him up, and then I called Danny and told them to get ready. I picked up Danny first, then let him drive to Mike's. I had two walkie-talkies with new batteries. We drove out to the cornfields, and everything looked tip-top. Danny dropped us, Mike and I made our way down to where the plants were, and the scene was looking better than good. It was just like we had left it, except we had little pot plants coming up all over. No animals were getting in. The plants were about three to four inches high. There were only a few pods that we had to reseed. We didn't have to water them after all the rain we had.

I gave Danny a radio check and heard a green light. I asked him to give us a half hour. He said, "Okay." Mike assembled the fence, and I spread my seeds out. It was so cool to know that in a few short months, we would be in weed heaven. Naturally, Mike and I were two deliriously happy boys.

I got a radio call. Danny was asking when we would be ready.

"In about ten minutes."

"Copy that."

We proceeded over to the pickup area. I received a call from Danny. I said we were ready for our ride. He pulled over, and we got in. He lit up a joint as he drove off, and he wanted to know everything. Mike filled him in and estimated that in three weeks, we would have to plant them in the field. Everyone was happy. I dropped off Mike. Danny and I socialized at the bar for a few hours, and then I took him home. I called Big G and let him know what we saw, and he was happy, too.

Well, about six weeks passed, and we were ready to go out and do some planting. We all got together, and Mike had gotten three army shovels. Big G drove us out in his van. The cornfields, like always, looked good on the first pass. Big G pulled over and let us out. I took one radio. We climbed over the little hill and down to our spot. It looked better and better every time I came to this place. The plants were about a foot tall and looking mighty. Now, it was planting time.

Mike, Danny, and I took a little stroll to see where we could stick the plants in the cornfield. As we were walking, I gave Big G a call on the radio and said we had a green light, and I would call him in a few hours. He said he copied that. We paced about four rows deep into the cornfield, and Mike said to plant one every four or five cornstalks—pull out a cornstalk and plant our weed in its place.

I sent Danny down this one row to pull cornstalks, and Mike and I would carry the pods over in boxes. The corn was four feet high already, and these fields were immense, so we decided to put a pile of rocks at our starting point. These cornstalks would grow even taller, and we didn't want to have to hunt for our weed plants. It would look a lot different in a few more months.

We filled two boxes and hoofed the pods over. Mike planted, and I brought more. After a few hours, Big G called over the radio. I said we had a green light, but we needed a few more hours. We were only about halfway through.

It was a hot, sunny day, and nothing was around—so quiet, so peaceful. Once we finished the planting, we collected all the cornstalks and hid them under some dense brush near the road. We set the shovel, fencing, and boxes near the pickup area and sat down. We did a little work that day, and we were feeling it, so we sat there for about a half hour before Big G called.

I picked up the radio, gave him the green light, and said we were ready. He said he was a few minutes away. We looked for him to come up the road. Danny said, "Here he comes," Big G pulled over, and we got in.

"It looks like you had a lot of fun."

I told him to fuck off. He just laughed, and we drove away. I guess it was the first week of June when we planted the plants in the field, and we would have to wait until harvest moon at the end of October to collect. That was assuming the weather held out, and it did.

At the end of July, we had to go back in and water the plants, the same in the middle of August. Each time, the picture was damn near perfect. They were getting tall, and we didn't have any problems, and soon it was October.

Big G, Danny, Mike, and I got together at the end of the month with some heavy-duty trash bags, and it was harvest time. Mike instructed Danny and me how to strip the plants in the field, which meant taking all the buds off and putting them into the bags before pulling the plants out of the ground. Another way of harvesting is to take the plants and hang them upside down, so more THC flows into the buds. Mike didn't want to do that. I just wanted to try my weed.

Once again, Big G pulled the van over, and we hopped out, and like always, I had the radio. We started toward where we thought we had the plants. The cornstalks had grown up, making everything looked different. We had to look for the pile of rocks.

We found the rocks. The plants were huge, and we were so f'ing happy. I gave Big G the green light and said we needed about three hours. He gave me a, "Copy that." We all split up and started to pull buds.

As I am writing this, looking back at that time, pulling those big buds off those plants was one of my favorite things I did. I tried something new and succeeded. I had never farmed in my life, and I knew I could make a fortune if I stuck with it. If I wanted to use this field again, I could. It was one hell of a growing spot. I never even looked back at that field again.

It took all of four hours before we finished. We took the fence down, gathered the buckets and everything we were taking with us over to the pickup area, and Big G was five minutes out. We saw him coming and got ready. He pulled over, and in short order, we put everything in the van, and off we went. In all the time we spent in that field, we never saw a car pass by.

We set up in one of Big G's garages, and Mike brought his triple beam scale from his house and some plastic baggies. We broke out a case of beer and unloaded the three large trash bags full of weed. We got to work weighing the weed and ended up with about ten-plus pounds each. We were all pleased, took our pot, and were on our ways.

I called my friend that had scavenged the pods for me, and he said he thought I had forgotten him. I assured him I would by no means do that. He scored five pounds at a good price, and I sold another two pounds within a week. The weed was good stuff.

MEETING GIL

Big G and I would go to this one club over behind the Reading bus terminal. We knew a few people that worked there, and one night, we met this guy named Gil. He had one beautiful girlfriend. Big G and I could not take our eyes off her, and Gil knew some of the people that Big G and I knew. We grew to know Gil and his girlfriend very well. Gil was a small-time thief, and he could get rid of hot items.

I ran my vitamin stores, and things were going well. Gil and I partied some but were not at all close buddies. About six months slipped away, and Big G and I took Gil out with us, and we made some money. It was a club up in northern Pennsylvania. We made a few grand each. After that, Gil was around a lot. We would use him now and then, but Gil would try to go out on his own. He could not do what Big G and I could. Not many people can.

THE ATLANTIC CITY STORE

Well, there I was in Atlantic City, looking for a place to put a third vitamin store. The year was '81 or '82, and Atlantic City was booming. Everyone was making money in that town. I found a little storefront at Florida and Arctic Avenue, and it took Christine and me about two weeks of hard work to get that store up and running.

After we signed the lease, the first thing I did was put an ad and a 10 percent coupon in the newspaper: *Your super stimulant vitamins store is open at Florida and Arctic*. I also put in our slogan: *Reduce while you maintain energy*, because the pills increased your heart rate and suppressed your appetite. In a few weeks, we added *Robin Eggs, Black Beauties, and an assortment of other stimulants, sleep aids, and vitamins* to my ad.

Nothing happened the first week. Christine and I painted and put up shelves, even installed glass showcases, and the next week, as we were stocking shelves, we had ten people come by in one day. We made $250 that day, and business progressed, day by day.

I guess we were there about a few weeks before we had our first special guest visitor. Little Nicky Scarfo, the head of the mob, came by when I was not there and looked around. He told Christine, "Good luck with the store." I never met the man, but he lived around the corner.

The business was going well for me, and I loved Atlantic City. Everything was great. It was summer 1982, and the Beach Boys were having a free concert. Zapper the Rapper came up from Texas to see it. We showed up three hours early to get an excellent spot. We put our cooler and three blankets down. We were about eighty feet from the stage. Then, I saw some people that I knew from Reading. They came over, and we introduced everyone to everyone. There was a girl there, Sandy, and she looked perfect. I gave her a nickname right there, Sandy Sandwich, and it stuck with her until she passed away. Nevertheless, we went swimming in the ocean, and we all had a lot of fun.

I got to know Sandy Sandwich personally and gave her a job in the Atlantic City store. She and Christine became good friends. I had a little apartment in the back of the Atlantic City store with a bed, a couch, a shower, and a TV. Sandy and Christine would stay in the apartment, and I traveled back and forth from Reading and the New Brunswick store. It was so nice. And then, I received a call from Big G. He wanted to have a powwow.

THE 1981 BANK JOBS

I headed back into Reading and gave Big G a call. We met over at his house. He asked what we had. I came clean. "I have two banks on the list up in Phillipsburg and Clinton, New Jersey. I have been waiting to do a bank, and it's time."

The next day, Big G and I got in touch with Gil and Bob and told them we needed them to come over to the house around 11:00 a.m. Once they arrived, we told them straight up: we were going to look at some banks on Sunday, and we wanted them to drive. We met at around 9:00 p.m. The drive up to Phillipsburg takes around an hour and a half; that would put us up there around 10:30 p.m. or 11:00 p.m.

We approached the first bank in Phillipsburg and drove by it, and it was excellent. We drove down, turned around, and pulled over, so we could get the walkie-talkies and the gloves out of the trunk. I hopped out, grabbed the gear out of the trunk, and got back in. I told Bob to drive, and I made Big G tell him where he wanted him to pull over. We were about a quarter mile from the bank, and Big G said, "That's far enough." It was so quiet around this area, not too much traffic. Big G, Gil, and I got out of the car and made our way over to the bank. We pulled our ski caps down over our faces.

Once we got over to the bank. We made our way over to the drive-up window, not looking at the drop box, but at the safes that hold the change. There were about five, and they looked like we could pop them open. We would not do this bank until Wednesday, when they filled up the safes with the exchanges from the weekend. I didn't like doing the drop box. It would take too long to open. The safes were hard enough. That put us in the hot zone for a long time, maybe hurting our chances of getting away with this job. We saw where the cameras were, and we went around to see if the front door had alarm clips. They did.

Now, we looked for a way into this bank without using the front door. In the front of the bank, at the bottom of the large window, was a square of glass. It was a narrow piece window, about a foot wide and four feet long. We could lie on the grass and work on it, and no one would be able see us. It would not take us any time at all.

Well, it was time to get out of there. We had seen everything we needed to see. We gave Bob a radio check, and he called us back right away. We told him we would be at the pickup spot in five minutes. He responded that he was ten minutes out. We said everything was green and ten was fine. We were at the pickup area for a short moment, and then Bob pulled over. We looked around for parking for this bank, and there was nothing that we could use. We had no choice but to let Bob drive on this one.

We made our way over to the next bank, about twenty minutes down the road in Clinton. When we got there, we noticed an apartment building within walking distance. Excellent—parking was no problem. Bob dropped us off where Big G told him to, and I told him to park and get the other radio out of the trunk. I added, "Make sure that no one sees you."

"Okay."

The boys and I made our way over to where we wanted Bob to keep lookout.

This was a choice lookout area. You could see any car coming up to the bank, about four blocks away. This was shaping up to be a great score, if it checked out okay. We signaled Bob with Big G's trusty pocket flashlight. He always had a light in his pocket. On and off, we showed Bob where we were. He walked up to us, and we told him to stay in this spot. Big G, Gil, and I pulled our caps down and walked over to the drive-up window.

We looked in and saw the safes behind the counter. They looked like we could pop them open, just like at the first bank. We saw the cameras and made our way over to the front door to look for alarm clips on the door. There were no clips. That made us happy. Back in those days, cops were not even looking at banks on their night patrols. Not many of them were being done, so there was no heat on them.

I called Bob to get the car and pick us up at the drop-off area. He came back over the radio: "I copy." Big G, Gil, and I walked over to the pickup area. Bob was there about the same time with the car. We got in, and Bob took off. We told Gil and Bob that we would leave at about the same time on Wednesday. When we got back to Reading, I said my goodbyes to Gil and Bob, a good night to Big G, and went to bed.

The next day, when I woke up, Big G had brought breakfast. We reviewed what we would need for the bank jobs. Big G asked me to pick up black spray paint for the cameras. He wanted to take the torch set, in case we saw something in there that we hadn't seen before. We collected everything we needed early in the day, so we were ready to go. When Gil and Bob arrived, right at 9:00 p.m., they didn't even come into the house. Bob drove and kept a CB radio and the scanner in the car.

We checked on the first bank around 11:00 p.m. Looked great. We passed by the bank in Phillipsburg, and it, too, was excellent, so we told Bob to find a place to get the tools and the radio out. He found a pretty pullover place, and we took out the in-tool bag with the radio and black spray paint inside, and a Johnson bar. I brought everything into the backseat and hopped back in the car. Bob took off for the drop-off area, pulled over, and Gil, Big G, and I jumped out. I handed Big G the Johnson bar and the radio, and I took the in-tool bag. I gave Gil the portable torch set. I felt good about this night. We pulled our ski caps down and ran over to the in window. I grabbed some tools to take it out.

Big G on lookout, Gil and I got to work on the window after a green light from Bob. It took me about half an hour to get the window out. I spray painted the cameras. Then, Big G came in, and we got to work. Gil stayed outside for the lookout. As I was working, Big G was shaking down the whole bank to make sure we didn't miss anything. He brought over some large bank bags and a bucket with wheels. I absolutely loved my job in those moments.

I cracked the first safe open with two screwdrivers and the Johnson bar. I put the large screwdrivers in the top corner of the safe and got that corner loose. Then, I slid the heavy Johnson bar in the opening and popped open the safe. There was a few thousand in this one. I moved to the next safe while Big G put the money in the bucket behind me. We did the same thing to the next three safes. It only took us about forty minutes to get all the safes open and the money out of them. We put all the tools away and moved everything to the window.

We had to make two trips from the bank to the pickup area. I guess we had about eight thousand. Like all the honorable institutions that we did, they always reported more to the insurance company than we take. We saw that a lot when we read about the jobs in the paper.

We gave Bob a call on the radio, "We have a green light, and we're ready."

"Copy that," he answered and told us he was a short drive out.

Then we saw a car approaching, giving us the high beam/low beam headlights. We gave him the flashlight on and off. He pulled over and popped the trunk. Boom. Done.

Bob asked us how it went.

"About eight thousand."

"Wonderful."

At this point, we had to decide if we were going to find a place to stash the money we had just made, because if we got stopped or busted at the other score and we didn't have the money on us, they couldn't put that score on us. We took a vote, and we decided to keep the money on us. We were off to Clinton.

We investigated the bank, and the conditions were still perfect. We took a little drive and repeated the drop-off routine, except this time, I handed Bob a radio because he would be out there on this one. He also had to carry the scanner with him.

We made our way over to the lookout and waited for Bob. It only took him about fifteen minutes to park and walk over. We asked him if he was ready for this job. He told us, "Yes," so Big G, Gil, and I started to walk over to the bank. We pulled our ski caps down, and I went around to the front door and began to remove the lock. It was easy—if you just cut the protective metal collar around the lock cylinder and twist with a pipe wrench, the part you put your key into unscrews. Then, you fit a screwdriver in, slip it to the right, and the locking bar moves to the right, too. When that happens, you just pull the door open, and you're in.

So, I did that, walked in, and sprayed the cameras with the black paint. We went around the counter, over to the safes under it. To our surprise, there was a safe you could not see behind the counter. It was a bigger, square-door safe. We looked for a bug on it—it was clean, but we would need the torch on this one. We decided we would do the little ones the same way I did at the first bank and get that money out first, just in case something went wrong. Bob came over the radio to check in. We gave him the green light and kept working. *If we get away with these two banks in one night,* I thought, *the FBI is going to be pissed off.*

Well, it was time to move the money and the tools out to the pickup area. We got a green light from Bob. Once there, we sent Bob to get the car. He came back in fifteen minutes. We put the money in the trunk. Looking at both piles, this did not seem like as much as we had gotten out of the first bank, but we would compare again in about two hours.

I told Bob to park the car but in a different spot. He said, "Okay." Fifteen more minutes ticked off, and we saw Bob coming. These towns were so quiet. The whole time we were working, there was no activity. And there was still no activity. That made me happy.

Big G, Gil, and I started to walk over to the bank with the in-tool bag and the torch. We got a green light from Bob. We went behind the hedge on the dark side of the bank and assembled the torch there: the acetylene gauge on the small acetylene tank, and oxygen gauge on the mini oxygen tank. Then, we hooked up the torch to the oxygen line and the acetylene line. We stowed the assembly back in the carrying bag to make it easier to handle. Now, we were set to do the job. We called Bob for a green light. We got a green light, and we went into the bank. I told Gil, "Stay outside and keep a good eye on things."

I used two screwdrivers in between the door and the side of the safe and pried precisely hard enough to see the round locking pins. I could clearly see three in total. I held the screwdrivers so Big G could see. He fired up the torch and melted a hole through the side of the safe at the top pin. We didn't make that much smoke, but we had to be careful because we didn't want to set off the fire alarm. We made the next hole, and that went well, also, but we had to turn off the torch while I dug out a punch and drove the pins back into the safe door. The pins fell into the door with only a few hits each. Big G fired up again, torched the last hole, and then immediately turned the torch off and set it down. I punched the last pin. Big G pulled on the door, and it came open.

I just loved this work. It's true. There was cash, traveler checks, and change. We pulled teller drawers with even more money. Now, we were in a rush to get out of there. We moved everything out of the bank to the dark side. We called Bob.

"Green light."

"Come over to help move everything over to the pickup area."

He came, we started back to the pickup area, and Big G pulled this money out of a teller's drawer, and he set off this red dye bomb!

We went running up this hill, and don't you know it—here comes a cop car! We barely made it into the woods and watched him pass, but you could see the smoke yet. The cop put his brakes on, but he didn't stop. We dashed for the car. I got the keys off Bob, opened the door, and popped the trunk. We threw everything inside the vehicle, and we took off. We made it down the road without seeing anyone, and we were thrilled that we didn't have a problem. We got back to the house by early morning and pulled everything out except the tellers' drawers and the tools. Once everything was in the house, we got the tellers' drawers out, and we set them on the side of the house where no one could see.

Three drawers had the red dye bombs in them yet. I told Big G to get the water hose, and we wetted them down. Then, I told them I was going to pull the money out and throw the dye bombs.

I threw one, two, three, and bam, bam, bam—they went off. The water didn't help. There was red smoke all over. Big G sprayed the smoke with water, and that seemed to improve after about ten minutes. Finally, everything calmed down. We got the money and put it in the house. We took the drawers and put them in the car.

Back inside, we started to split up the money. By the time we were done, we had about twenty thousand in traveler's checks and somewhere between fifteen and twenty thousand in cash.

We told Gil and Bob goodbye, and they left. Big G and I stuffed our money away, and we moved the car out to the stash area. I put on some gloves, grabbed a hammer, and smashed the drawers. When I was done, you couldn't tell what they were. We loaded the drawer scraps into my car and took a ride to dump them where no one would find them.

That was the last time I would work with Gil. He was an okay worker, but the connection just wasn't that strong. Gil was going out with other people I knew, and I do not believe Big G went out with him after that, either.

THE HOUSE IN OCEAN CITY

I wanted to move out of Reading, and I was looking down at the shore. I loved Atlantic City. The store was doing well, but the one in Reading was the moneymaker, with it being near the outlet stores (and the outlet stores brought in the buses). That store was the king. But Atlantic City was the place you wanted to be. I got to know many people down there, and we had a lot of fun.

I met Mr. Atlantic City, Skinny D'Amato. He once owned the 500 Club and would have the Rat Pack over to his home. I got to know his daughter more than I knew him. I only met him about twice, but his daughter would come over and hang out sometimes. Mike's father came down, and he knew several people in Atlantic City. He was selling slushy-making machines that combined ice and fruit mix. He was the first to bring the slushy machine to town. He had a meeting with Steve Wynn, who I wanted to meet so bad. Wynn had this big—very big—gold nugget in his casino, the Golden Nugget. In truth, I would stand and stare at that nugget for hours at a time. I genuinely loved that nugget, and that became my favorite casino.

I finally rented this house in Ocean City, a three-bedroom about one block from the ocean. Christine and I moved in with some furniture that I bought. I kept one bedroom empty because I had a plan for that room. I will tell you the idea later.

Days were going great. I was only working the stores, not doing night work. I would drive to the New Brunswick and the Reading stores once a week, restock, and pick up the money. Christine and I would just hang out around the house.

I made a call to Zapper the Rapper for his cousin Mack's phone number. I called Mack up and asked him if he could get me any magic mushrooms. He told me he would get back to me in a few days. I went out and got a book on how to grow these types of mushrooms. You could get about $150 for one ounce. I guess I had grown bored running stores. I needed something fun to do.

Mack called back, and he told me he would send me the spores from the mushrooms. It was easier to ship than deliver, and no heat. I told him to send it.

A few days later, a letter from Mack came in the mail. He lived in Texas. I honestly love Texas. I opened the envelope, and there was a letter and an itty-bitty, sealed plastic bag. I couldn't make out what was in it, but I knew it was the spores—little black spores, millions and millions in this small plastic bag. That made my day.

Now, I had to go out and buy plastic gloves, plastic containers, stuff to keep everything sterile, a microscope so I could see the spores, and tools to separate them. I then went and got soil mix with fertilizer. After all that, I went out and picked up four workbenches, one and a half sheets of plywood, two ten-foot pieces of six by six, and lumber nails. I hammered the plywood to the six by sixes. I put the assembly on the four workbenches. I lined it with plastic, and the growing area was ready to go. Okay, now it was time to try to grow mushrooms, or as I called it, grow fungus.

I took the spores and mixed them with their food to get a culture. I got my microscope and the plastic container out. I took the liquid nutrient out and the bag of spores and made sure that everything was sterile. I put plastic gloves on and set the spore bag under the scope. I opened the bag, scooped up the spores, and put them into the plastic container with the liquid nutrients in it. I did this three times. Now, I had to wait a week to see if this process worked, and I hoped by the week's end, I would have fungus growing.

TIME FOR THE ROAD TRIP

I received a call from Big G, who told me we must go on a week-long road trip and to get Danny. I told him I would check on my other stores and be able to go in two days.

I called Danny. He was ready to hit the road. I said, "Good. I will pick you up in a few days." I took care of what I needed to take care of, and two days later, I called Danny to say I would be there in a few hours.

I then called Big G and told him I would see him in a few hours. He told me we would take his car and my van. I said that was cool. He told me he had some news for me, and it was not good—something to do with Gil and Bob. I picked up Danny, and we met Big G. When he pulled up, he told me to get in the car, and Danny had to drive the van. We were going to go out the turnpike to I-81 and then head south. I could tell that Big G was not himself. We started to drive, and he said to me that Gil got busted trying to sell hot stuff to an undercover cop and turned over on Bob.

I knew Bob well, and somehow, I knew Gil would tell the FBI about the banks we did with him to stay out of jail. I knew the FBI only had Gil's word at this time, and that was not enough to take us to court, but I also knew they were watching us. I asked Big G where we were going. He told me south, and we didn't say too much for a few hours. It was hard to believe this was going on in my life. Things had been going perfect for me. And now this?

Well, a few days later, I found myself down in the good old state of Louisiana, in the city of Baton Rouge. We played in that city for a few days. We looked around and didn't see anything we liked, so we moved over to Lake Charles, and I just fell in love with that town. We stayed around there for three days. We didn't see anything we liked there, either, so we moved up to Alexandria and found a club we liked.

We drove around, found parking, and looked at the score again. From there, we went north and rented a room about one hour away. It was Saturday, and we were ready to make some money. We would use the van and bring the car down near the score in case we needed it.

We brought the tools into the room and wiped everything down, put new batteries in everything. Then, we turned the scanner on and put in the frequency for Alexandria. We must have listened to the scanner for four hours, and there was no activity at all. I hoped this was a good sign. We put the tools back in the van and took it easy until Sunday night. Big G and I didn't talk about Gil, because until we knew what was going on, there was nothing we could do.

Well, on Sunday at about 10:30, it was time to go. Big G drove the van, and I went with him. Danny followed in the car. We got down near the score, and Danny parked the car and got in the van. We drove past the score—very appealing. Danny and I got ready to exit the van. I grabbed the scanner and in-tool bag. Danny got the CB radio. Big G turned around and pulled over near the score to drop us off and leave. We made our way over to the lookout area, and we would wait until Big G got back.

Well, a half hour passed, and then one hour. Now, I was getting worried. I knew something had happened to Big G. Danny wanted to make a move—either do the job or go to the car. I told him we would stay here for one more hour then make our way over to the car. About twenty minutes later, I saw Big G walking. He got to the lookout area and told us that he lost the van. "A cop put his lights on, and I pulled over and ran." There were no tools in the van, and it was not hot.

I asked him, "Why didn't you just see what the cop wanted?"

"I didn't want to take a chance and end up in a Louisiana jail because of Gil."

Well, we made our way over to the car. Danny jumped in the driver's seat and popped the trunk. Big G and I put the tools in the trunk and got out of there. We made it back to the room with no problem. I had to call the Reading police and tell them my van was stolen but would wait until I got back to Reading. I could say I'd been on vacation and didn't know how long it'd been missing. We rested and then got busy heading north.

I was a little mad that Big G didn't try to save the van, but if Gil did rat, I wouldn't like being locked up in Louisiana, either. Well, two days passed, and we were up in Kentucky, just taking our time, looking around, hoping to make money. We went into this little town and passed a jewelry store. Big G and I went in and took a look. It had no bugs and a little square-door safe. The jewelry was gorgeous, and they had some gigantic rings. We took a quick look and got out of there. We got back in the car, and off we went.

We told Danny it looked tiptop, so we looked for parking and a drop-off area. We found what we needed and headed out of there to look for a room. A little over an hour away, we found a suitable place. Danny went in and made the reservation. We knew the tools were good to go, so we only brought the scanner into the room. We programmed it for the town where the jewelry store was. We rested until about 10:00 p.m.

Danny drove this time, and it took a little over an hour before we were there. We drove by, and the scene looked normal, just right. Danny drove to where we could get the tools out. He pulled over, popped the trunk, and Big G and I got the tools out and stepped back into the car. Danny drove to the drop-off area, and Big G and I got out. We made our way over to the lookout area and waited for Danny.

It took him a little time. I was getting a little nervous, and then I saw him coming. Big G and I got ready to get the "in" to the store. We came up to the store and asked Danny for a green light, got it, and made our move to the back door. I had two screwdrivers in my hand and popped it open within a minute. We were in.

Big G headed to the front of the store to take a look. I pulled a hammer out of the bag and hit the dial off the safe. I took a punch out, gave it two or three hits, then moved the safe handle, and the damn thing came open. Big G asked for a green light. Danny came back and said, "You have a green light." We dragged a bucket out of the back room and started putting the jewelry in. After a few minutes, I was ready to get out of there. Big G asked Danny for a green light.

Danny told us everything was green. We opened the back door, and out we went. Once we made it over to the lookout area, we sent Danny to get the car. That it only took about a half hour to get in and do the safe was amazing. We moved to the pickup area, and Danny was there in ten minutes. He popped the trunk. We put everything in and hopped in the car.

We drove all night back to Reading, taking turns over the ten-hour trip. We put the car in the stash place. Danny got his car, and we put everything in it. We went to Big G's apartment and laid the loot out on the floor. There was about fifty thousand to seventy thousand dollars' worth, so we would get about fifteen to twenty thousand for the jewelry. That would help if we needed attorney money if Gil turned into a rat.

Danny went home. I gave Christine a call to come and pick me up. Big G would keep the jewelry, show it to a few guys, and accept the best offer. Christine was a few hours out, so I went out for some beer and just took it easy until she arrived.

Christine made it to Big G's apartment, and as we said our goodbyes, I told Big G to keep me up to date on Gil.

BACK TO THE HOUSE IN OCEAN CITY

Christine and I made it back to the house, and I could not wait to see how my mushrooms were doing. I hurried to my fungus farm and put on plastic gloves. I uncovered the microscope, put the plastic container under it, and popped open the tub. To my surprise, nothing happened. I opened the other container—same thing.

I would have to sterilize all this equipment and start the whole process over. I cleaned up, putting everything away because I had to call the cops and tell them my van was missing. I told them I was at my other store in New Brunswick for a little over a week. I had just gotten home a short while ago, and my van was not where

I had parked it. I also told them that my girlfriend and I were the only people that had keys to the van, that she was the one that took me to where I parked it, and, "Needless to say, the van wasn't there. That's why I am on the phone with you."

They told me to come to the station and make a report, so I had Christine take me. I was in the lion's den full of cops for one and a half hours. After that, Christine and I went home and had some good sex. Then, I told her that I'd had enough of this day, and I was going to go to sleep.

The next day, I woke up and got my stuff together to try to get the mushrooms growing again. I put rubber gloves on, and then I laid the groundwork—the sterilized containers, the mushroom spores, the nutrients, the microscope, and the special tools. I opened up the containers and spores, looked at them under the microscope, and then scraped some into a bin. Then, I added some nutrients and put the lid on. I did that two more times, exactly like the first one. I hadn't known that trying to grow a fungus was so technical and fun. I laid around the house for a few days, and I loved it. It was spring out, and I was one block from the ocean.

BAD NEWS FROM BIG G

Well, as you know, happiness only lasts for a fraction of time. I got a call from Big G, who notified me that he needed to see me. I asked him, "Do you have good news or bad news?" He told me he had good and bad news. I said, "I'll see you in a day or so. I have to go to North Jersey and stock the store and do payroll, and I will be in Reading to do that store in a day or so."

He said, "That's cool."

The North Jersey store was going strong, making me money. I said my goodbyes, and I headed to Reading store, the mint. It kicked ass. I did what I had to do there, and I found a payphone. I called Big G and told him I was ready to meet. He wanted to meet at Chef's Lounge in twenty minutes. It was early in the afternoon. "I'll be there," I said, and when I pulled up, I noticed Big G's car outside. I went in. The owner and two or three other people were there. Big G and I walked to the back, and he handed me an envelope.

"There's $4,900 in that envelope," he said. "That's from the jewelry score. Now, order a large drink, because the news I'm about to tell you is not too good."

I ordered a double Jack and Coke. I drank it right down and ordered another one.

"Gil just got picked up for burglarizing a penthouse apartment, and Bob was picked up, too," he told me. Now, Gil was facing *two* burglary charges. Then Big G said, "He might rat on us to save his ass."

"Did Gil make bail?"

"Yes, he did."

"Did Bob make bail, too?"

"Uh-huh."

We knew that Bob would not rat on us, but Gil was a little bullshit thief, and I knew he would rat. This was not good news. It would just be a matter of time.

The state had him now, but what he knew about Big G and me would set him free. He would get a sweet deal from the FBI when he told them about the bank jobs we had just done in New Jersey. Well, at this time, they only had his word and no evidence. I just wanted to go home and analyze all this.

I told Big G, "Goodbye," got in my car, and went home. That night, I could not sleep. I was trying to imagine what the state or FBI's next move might be. The only thing I could come up with was, *Will they bug our phones and follow us, or go after a weak link that could help their case?*

THE STATE ARRESTS GARY

A few days later, the state made their move. They picked up Gary and charged him with racketeering. That's when you take illegal money and put it into a legal business. What business? D&G Vitamins. Gary was my partner when I opened the first shop, and he had borrowed some money from Sal, the gangster.

When Gary told me he wanted to get out of the vitamin business, I decided I would pay back Sal fully. When I heard that D&G Vitamins was involved in Gary's case, I knew that they were trying to find something against me. They were hoping that Gary could tell them something, but he was a standup guy, and he wouldn't tell them anything.

Big G and I worked on getting Gary bail. We sent word to him in jail to hold tight, and that things would be okay. He sent word back and told us everything was fine. In about a week and a half, we were able to get Gary out on bail. The day he got out, Big G and I went to see him. He confirmed that they wanted to know about me—whether I knew Gil and where I had gotten the money to open the D&G Vitamins. He said, "I refused to answer any questions."

I said, "That's good. They must not have enough evidence to come after me." They were looking for someone that could help get evidence against me and help flesh out Gil's testimony.

I told Gary, "Get in touch with Sal and have him meet with your attorney. Tell him about the money you borrowed from Sal to start up D&G Vitamins with me. But do not tell the prosecutor until you really have to." I wanted the state to think they had Gary where they wanted him for as long as possible. I said my goodbyes and went home.

BACK TO OCEAN CITY

Well, I got home, just taking it easy, and I remembered about the mushrooms. I went in the back bedroom and dug out my plastic containers. All three had the puffy, white goo growing in them. Now, at this time in my life, I didn't want any more problems. I just sat there looking at the fungus, thinking that in about a week or so, I could have a whole room full of magic mushrooms. I could probably have about five pounds, and at $150 an ounce, that would give me about ten to twelve thousand dollars. I knew in my heart that I was going to need this money. But, on the other hand, if the FBI came and kicked down my door, the newspaper would read, *A bank burglar was arrested, and the FBI found a room full of magic mushrooms growing in his house.* That would not look very good in court.

It was about 7:00 p.m., and I decided I could not let that happen. By midnight, I had two buckets out and was starting to put the fertilizer in the buckets. I then took the compost out my back door, went to my next-door neighbor, and began to put it around his rose bushes. I did that for a few hours and got rid of all the fertilizer. Then, I took apart all the other equipment. I put all the wood in my van and took it to a dumpster. I cleaned up the room spotless. I got rid of the spores, put the microscope away, and finished around 4:00 a.m.

I woke up the next day at around 11:00 a.m. Christine would be home in a few hours from her mother's, whom she visited after she closed the Atlantic City store. I would tell her what was going on. I knew I would have to move around a lot starting now, and I didn't know what to do with the stores.

Christine walked in, and I told her what was going on. I said, "I will move around so they can't find me. You better pack up your things. You're moving back in the Atlantic City store." I would have someone move the bigger items in for her.

I started packing my things up, and she did the same. I took her to Atlantic City on Sunday, and no one was around. We loaded her stuff, and I took off.

. . . .

PART V

ON THE RUN

I needed a room in Reading. A friend of mine owned the in-town motel. I went there but didn't tell him that I was having trouble.

"I might need this room for a few weeks."

"Whatever you need," he assured me.

I stayed in that motel for a few weeks, and nothing happened—no FBI, no state cops, no city cops, and no word from Gary's attorney. I would still go to my stores, do payroll, and do the stock, but no one would know when I would come. Then, I got a call from Gary, and he said, "I had to make the move regarding the testimony from Sal, the gangster, and the state dropped all charges."

That made me very happy. That told me I had some time and took some pressure off. I gave Big G a call. He mentioned that he'd heard about Gary and was happy. He asked me if I wanted to go to work.

"Not at this time, but I will give you a call if I need to work."

We said our goodbyes. I knew that this would be a lousy time if one of us got busted.

BIG G GOT BUSTED AGAIN

A few more weeks passed, and Big G got busted with all the tools in the car. He was going to do a score, and they pulled him over because he looked suspicious. They confiscated the radios, scanner, torch set, and in-tool bag. Now, the state and the FBI had the evidence they were looking for. Once I heard that, I knew that they were coming.

Big G made bail, but the FBI was there to re-arrest him for three bank burglaries, two in New Jersey and one in Delaware. They arrested Bob for the same jobs. Now I knew, in a week or so, after they talked to Big G and Bob to see if they would rat, they would come after me. But I would not be the easy one to catch. I knew the longer I could run from this, the better off I would be. If Bob and Big G didn't say anything, the FBI would have a hard time convicting me with the evidence they had—just Gil's testimony saying I was there. I knew I would have to find an unknown place to lay low for a few months.

Big G and Bob made bail on the bank charges. A few days later, I called for a meeting with Big G. We met over at Danny's apartment. The first question I asked him was, "Do you think the garage," or stash house, as I knew it, "is safe?" I needed to know this because we had two more sets of burglary tools there. I added, "What are you going to do?"

Big G said, "I don't know right now."

"Come with me."

"I will let you know."

We said our goodbyes, and he went home, and I could tell that he was feeling a lot of pressure.

THE HAMBURG HIDEOUT

Well, I gave Zeb a call and told him I needed a place to lay low for a little while. He told me to come on up. He had a cabin in Hamburg with three bedrooms. It was on five acres of land, and he had a few horses that he took care of. I moved some things into the top-floor bedroom. It was the start of summer, and I knew the FBI would never look for me there.

Well, about two weeks went by, and I was on my way to the store in Atlantic City. I pulled over and called Big G from a payphone. He told me the FBI wanted me really bad. They were trying to get him and Bob to rat on me, and they had offered him an impressive deal. I asked, "Did you take it?"

"Me and Bob told the FBI we have nothing to say to them."

I knew they would not say anything. Bob and Big G were hardcore men, and they had been down this road before. I told Big G that I would call him in a few days but didn't tell him where I was living. He gave me a new phone number to call from a new phone booth, and we said our goodbyes.

I made it down to Atlantic City. I parked my car far away from the store and walked. I walked into the store, and Christine was stunned that I was there.

"The FBI was just here about fifteen minutes ago."

I asked her to give me the money, and she did. I let her know that I would bring her some stock for the store, then off I went. I knew the FBI would not stop until they got me, and they had a lot of money and people. I got my car and headed to the Hamburg hideout. If I were to get stopped for any reason—a red light, a stop sign, speeding—that would be it for me. Off to the big house I would go. Needless to say, I would not drive over the speed limit, and I became the best driver in Pennsylvania and New Jersey for as long as I was on the run.

I got back to the cabin with no problems, and my friend, Zeb, was there. I said, "Look, I have some problems, and I just need time to sort them out."

A few days later, I decided that I would close down the store in Atlantic City. Move all the stock up to the Reading store. I also decided to sell my stores to my mother before the heat got too bad.

A few days passed. The store in Atlantic City was closed, and the stock was in the Reading store. I sent Christine back to her mother's and told her I would call in a few days. I went to see my mother and my stepfather, and I told them I had some troubles.

"It might be good for you if you buy my stores in New Brunswick and Reading." I proposed six grand for the stock and the stores. "You'll make that back in a few weeks."

They took the deal, and they had the money in the house. My stepfather's name was Brandy Pasco, and he was one hell of a man. He went into the bedroom and came out with the money. He drew up an agreement, I put my John Hancock on it, and he gave me the money. I told them goodbye and got out of there. It was more dumb luck that I was not caught at my mother's or any of my stores. My mother lived in Reading.

The Hamburg hideout was only forty minutes away, and I had about thirty thousand to my name. I had six on me and about twenty-four up in the bedroom at the cabin. If I laid low, my cash could last me for about a year or so. And you know, back in 1983, thirty thousand was a lot of money. I figured I would just ride horses and hang out at home. Someone would have to drive me around. So, I gave Danny B. a call.

"Whatever you need, I'll help you with."

"You'll have to pick me up at Zeb's house."

"Just let me know what you want me to do."

I must say that the Hamburg hideout turned into one hell of a good time for me, even though I was on the run. Zeb, Danny, Christine, Sandy, and I would party and ride horses all the time. This one time, Zeb, Christine, Sandy, and I went to the Hamburg watershed, where the town got their drinking water, a half mile away from the house. We walked up the trail and sat down near the water for a while. It was about ninety degrees, so we all decided to undress and get into that water to cool off.

We'd been swimming for about an hour with our birthday suits on and big smiles when, up on top of the watershed, I saw a police car pull up and look down on us. *This is just great,* I thought. *How would that look in court?* "We arrested Mr. Johnson swimming in the nude in the Hamburg drinking water with two nude girls and another male that was also nude."

Well, we got the hell out of there and made it back to the hideout, but we could see the cops driving around the area. That was very dumb of me, but then again, I was not exactly considered an Einstein.

The months changed, and fall came. I was not doing anything, and the FBI was not bugging people as much as they had been before

BOB AND BIG G TRIAL

I guess enough time passed that Big G and Bob were going to trial, and they testified that they had nothing to do with the bank burglaries in New Jersey. Nevertheless, they were found guilty. The courts dropped the one in Delaware for lack of evidence. Sentencing was in two weeks, so I reached out to Big G.

"Now that you lost your trial, why don't you come on the run with me?"

"I just want this to be over."

He was desperate and told me the FBI was all over him everywhere he went because they were hoping that Big G would lead them to me. We needed a new communication plan. So, I gave Big G a new phone booth number, and from then on, I would call his sister when I needed to talk to him. She would relay instructions to him about what I wanted him to do. Big G would call Danny B. when he needed me. We said our goodbyes and wished each other good luck.

It was then time for Big G and Bob to be sentenced. The next day, Big G went to court with Bob. I would have to wait until the newspaper came out to find out what happened to them, like if they had to go to jail once they received their sentence right there and then. So, I bought a newspaper and found out they got seven and a half to fifteen years, and they immediately put them in jail. Big G and Bob had asked the judge for a little time to get their affairs order, but the judge had said, "No."

I knew Big G and Bob would send me a letter in a few days letting me know how to contact them, and I would send some money. About three weeks went by before Big G's sister gave me a call to say that she had a letter from him. I went to her house and read the message. Big G and Bob would be going to the Lewisburg Penitentiary. He gave me his and Bob's federal numbers and the address to the prison. I would have one of the girls send them a letter and money orders.

I called Sandy up and went to see her. I gave her two three-hundred-dollar money orders and the other information, so she could send Big G and Bob what they needed. I gave her a few hundred also for her troubles. I told her that she would have to do this for us for a few months. She said, "Whatever Big G and you need, I'll help."

GETTING ARRESTED

As you know, time and money go faster than you think. It was July of 1984. I had a few thousand left, and I knew I needed to get a crew together. I would use four men at all times.

I talked to Danny, who was my number one driver, a favorite friend over the years. I asked him if he would be interested in going out and doing some night work.

He said, "Anytime you're ready, I'm with you."

I also asked Zeb, and he told me he would give it a try.

I said, "We'll talk again, soon."

Then, I gave a call to this guy who had done a few things together with Danny, and he told me he was in. His name was

Robert R. I had only worked with this guy one time before, and I did not trust him. That was my feel, and, you'll see, I was right.

I would put Zeb at one end and Danny at the other as lookouts. That way, I would have everything covered while I was in the hot zone, working on making money. After a few days, I decided that Danny and I should go to the stash house and check if everything we needed was there, and if we lacked something, we would pick it up. I had been keeping up with the rent for this place but had not been there in months. We got to the stash house and went right in. For the first half hour, easily, I was nervous about being there. We went over everything: the scanners, the CB radios, the in-tools, the torch set. Everything I needed was there.

I said, "Now, we have to go on the road and look for the right scores."

He asked when we would go, and I told him to drive me home. Once there, I went to my room, dug out my list of the scores that Big G and I had found. The only problem was I didn't know what Big G had done. I had been on the run for almost a year, and I was not doing any night work.

At this point, I put the list back in its hiding place, got my Pennsylvania map out, and started looking for an area where we could make money. I decided that we would go up around Berwick, Bloomsburg, and Danville. That was a phenomenal area to make money. I had always been lucky up there.

The next day, Danny and I hit the road. About two and a half hours later, we were up in the Berwick area, and we didn't see anything that I liked. We drove to the Bloomsburg area, through the town, and we didn't like anything there, either. So, we went to Danville, and there was what we were looking for—a fire company. There were about ten cars in the lot and a lot of trash in the dumpster. I got out of the car, walked over to the dumpster, and saw many of the signs that made the score primo. I got in the car and told Danny to head back to Reading. We found what we were looking for. On our way out of town, we found an ideal drop-off area. We could get to it by railroad tracks that also ran to the back of the fire company. We could not ask for anything more. This was the first score I had done in a long time, and it could not have been more perfect.

As Danny and I were driving back to Reading, I said, "You and Zeb will be the lookouts. I don't take any chances and have to take the new guy with me." Robert would be by my side so that I could keep my eye on him. Danny agreed with me, and a few hours later, we were back in Reading. I told him I would call him and let him know when we would meet.

A few days later, I called everyone to a meet up at the Hamburg hideout. Once there, I told them that the score would be a fire company that Danny and I had found up in Danville. It was Wednesday. I told everyone to meet back at 1:00 p.m. on Friday. We would go up a day early, take a look at it during the day, and again at night. That way, if someone saw us, it would give them a day to forget us. I asked if everyone was in. They all said, "Yes."

Then, I told everyone it was beer thirty and time to go to the bar. There was a little bar we went to in the town of Hamburg. We went in, and I got the first three or four rounds. Danny took me home, dropped me off, and went back to the bar.

Before you knew it, it was Friday. Danny and I woke up around 6:00 a.m., went and got the tools out of the stash house, and returned to the hideout. By 12:30, everyone was there. We were on the road by 1:00. It took us around three hours to get up in the Danville area. We inspected the two lookout areas. I showed Zeb where I wanted him to stand and look out for unwanted people. Then, we circled to the other lookout area, and I showed Danny where I wanted him to stand. We then drove by the drop-off area, where Robert, Zeb, and I would get out with all the tools before Zeb walked back to his spot.

Now, it was time to look at the score, and at 4:00 p.m., the fire company was full. We all liked that. We went by where Danny would park the car, and everyone loved the spot. Then, we drove out of town and looked for a decent motel. We drove up to Rt. 80, and in Buckhorn, there was a huge truck stop and a motel. We all knew this would be a sterling place. I went in and got the rooms under a fake name. I told them we would be there until Monday morning.

Zeb and I stayed in one room, Danny and Robert, in the other. We put the CB radios and scanner in my room. I put the frequency crystal in the scanner for the cops and the fire co. in and around Danville. It was about 6:00 p.m., and we would take a ride around the whole job site around 9:00 p.m. I sent Danny out for food. He came back in about one hour. We ate and lay around until 9:00 p.m. We got in the car and went and saw everything again. I had a good feeling about this score.

We went into town, and no one even gave us a look. We said our goodnights. I listened to the scanner, and there were just regular affairs going on, and that was not much. I went and lay down around 1:00 a.m. Danny and Robert came over to my room at about 10:00 a.m.

The next day, around 1:00 p.m., we went out and just looked around a few more towns that were in the area. We went around the score around 7:00 p.m., and everything was beautiful. For a Saturday evening, it was doing good business. We got something to eat and then headed back to the room. We tried not to be seen too much around the motel and the town of Danville. We stayed in our rooms and took it easy. After spending all day together, we all wanted time to relax. Tomorrow was the big day. I felt we would walk with around $10,000. That would be $5,000 each, minus expenses. I projected, at the most, with a hard safe to open, we would only be in the hot zone for about three hours.

Zeb was watching TV, and I was playing with the scanner. There was not much coming through the scanner, and that made me very happy. I knocked off around 1:30 a.m. The next day, Danny and Robert came over about 11:00 a.m. I sent Danny out to get food, and Robert, Zeb, and I just relaxed some more in my room. Danny came back with the food. We ate and assessed the plan again: load all the tools up around 12:30 a.m., the torch set, radios, and in-tool bag.

Well, 12:30 a.m. came fast, so we loaded up the car. It was hot out, July of 1984. We started to head to the drop-off area. We got to the train tracks around 1:15 a.m., and the scene was looking good, so we went down the road, stopped, got the tools into the car, and headed back to the drop-off area.

Things were still looking nice. Danny pulled over, and Zeb, Robert, and I got out with the tools. I left a walkie-talkie with Danny so that he could communicate with us, and he pulled off. We walked down the railroad tracks a little and stashed the torch set by the tracks. We got the radios out and turned them on. Zeb headed to his lookout. Robert and I were on standby until we heard from Danny and Zeb. About fifteen minutes later, we heard from Zeb and then Danny. They called for a radio check, and I asked them for a green light. They both gave me the green light. I told them to be on their toes.

At that time, Robert and I started making our way to the back of the fire company. I asked for a green light, and they gave me a green light. As always, getting the "in" was the most dangerous time in the hot zone. I got out the large screwdrivers and told Robert to carry the in-tool bag. We went up a little hill from the train tracks and made our way around the other side. I saw an easy door I wanted to try.

I was trying to get the "in" when I got a call from Zeb. He told us to look out. "This cop came out of nowhere."

As he was telling me this, the cop turned into the fire company and saw Robert and me. He jumped on the gas and was flying down the side of the building. Robert and I started to run toward the back of the building. The door we were trying to get open was in the middle, and it was a long building. We got to the back of the building and headed to the little hill before the train tracks. By this time, the cop was on us. Robert ran down the hill and started going down the tracks. I made it halfway down the slope and sprained my ankle pretty bad.

The cop jumped out of his car, ran up to me with his gun out, and told me to get on the ground. I did, and he put the handcuffs on me. He helped me up, walked me over to the cop car, and put me in the back. Then, he called in to the police station and asked for backup. Two other cop cars showed up at the fire company. Two of the cops went down the hill, and about fifteen minutes later, I saw them come back with the in-tool bag and radios. I hoped they didn't find the torch set.

At this point, everyone was supposed to make their way over to the parking area, get in the car, go to the motel, clean out the room, and head back to Reading. Well, forty minutes elapsed. The cop started to ask me my name. I told him I was not saying anything. I wanted to talk to an attorney. He then asked if I was trying to be a tough guy.

"No, sir."

I didn't want them to know my name or that I was from Reading. If they stopped any of my men, who all had Reading addresses on their driver licenses, they would put them with me. The cop started up the car and headed down to the station. They took me out of the car and put me in a cell. At this point, I didn't know if Danny, Zeb, or Robert had gotten away. If they did what they were told, they'd be halfway back to Reading.

A few hours had wasted away, and they pulled me out of my cell and took me down to be booked. I knew at this time I had to give them my name and address. If I lied to them, I would be charged with falsifying a statement. By now, Danny, Zeb, and Robert would be back in Reading. The cops asked me my name, and I told them Johnson and my mother's address in Reading. I then told them I had nothing else to say except that I needed to see a doctor and talk to an attorney. They put me back in the cell.

I guess it was about 5:00 a.m. Monday morning when they came and took me to the hospital. They took an X-ray of my right foot. I just had a nasty sprain. They moved me back to the police station put me in the same cell as before. The cop and I didn't say a word to each other.

Around 10:00 a.m. on August 1, 1984, they took me to the courthouse and charged me with burglary, criminal attempt, possession of instruments of crime, criminal trespass, and criminal conspiracy. They didn't set the bail, because the FBI was filing a detainer for three bank burglaries, two of them in New Jersey and one in Delaware. They took me to Danville County Jail. I didn't see any of my men in jail when I got there. That's when I knew they had gotten away.

I lay down to rest a few hours, and then I heard a voice that I knew. I saw Zeb, Danny, and Robert coming down the hall. Stunningly, they put Robert in my cell, and they put Danny and Zeb in the cell next to me. I told Danny and Zeb we would talk when we didn't have people around us. I sat down with Robert.

"What happened?"

"When I got to the parking area, the car was gone. So, I'm walking to the motel…."

He was about four or five miles out of Danville when a cop spotted him. The cop let the dog loose, and that was it for him. I asked him where they got Danny and Zeb. He told me he didn't know; they kept them apart. I just sat back in my bed. I could not believe it—they all got busted.

A few hours later, they let us out to eat lunch. We all got our food and sat down together. I asked Zeb what happened. He told me that when he got to the car, Danny got behind the wheel and drove by the score not once but three times. He told me Danny would not do what he was told—and that was to not drive by the score. Zeb then said to me that after the third time, the cops pulled Danny over and arrested them. I looked at Danny and told him he just got Zeb, Robert, and himself busted. He didn't say anything.

We ate and went back to our cells. One of the inmates cleaning the floor slid a newspaper into my cell. We were all over the front page. The paper said that they got all the tools, the torch set, the radios, the in-tool bag, basically all the gear in the motel room. I suspected that in a day or so, they would get a call from the motel manager, and they would get the property we had in the room. Without a doubt, I was mad as hell that all of us had gotten busted, but in a way, I was glad it was coming to an end for me. Being on the run with the FBI on your ass is no fun. Well, I'd had enough of this day, so I called it a night.

I was right—the motel manager saw our pictures in the newspaper and called the cops. They went to the room and found more radios and incriminating evidence that would only help the state case against me.

PREPARING MY DEFENSE

A few days passed, and I got a letter from Sandy; it was great to hear from her. She helped me the most at this time in my life. She was my connection to the outside world. I sat for a few days to figure out what I needed her to do. I had to communicate with her and not let anyone know what I was asking her to do. So, I sat down and made a new alphabet for us. It looked Arabic. I kept a copy, and just waited for a few days for the right time to mail it.

Back then, we could seal our letters, and I just had to believe that no one would get a copy of our alphabets.

I sent the letter out, and in a few days, I got a letter back from Sandy in our coded language. I asked her how things were going out there, and I told her I needed her to write to a friend named Paul in Graterford Penitentiary. This friend had roughly eight more years to do, and I knew he would help me out if he could. I also had her write a letter Big G to find out his appeal status. Lastly, I asked her to go to the Reading library to see if they had a book on how to write motions and appeals at the federal level.

Time passes no matter where you are. Two weeks went by, and I got a letter from Sandy and a package. By this time, I had been moved to my own cell. I read the letter with my coded alphabet. I had to do this after lockdown, once I was alone. In her letter, she told me Big G was doing well, and his appeal was still in court. She then said Paul had instructed her to send me this law book, a how-to on federal motions and appeals. She told me the FBI was asking people around town about me, maybe compiling some kind of profile. She wished me luck and said she would write again. I destroyed her letter and put my code back in a safe place. I then opened up this law book and sat there trying to understand what I was looking at. I knew I would have to learn about the law if I was going to ever get out of jail at a young age.

Meanwhile, Zeb made bail within a few days. Danny, Robert, and I would see each other a few hours a day. They moved Robert up to the upper level of the jail. I told Danny this was not good. Then, he got out of jail on bail, too, and I knew he was going to turn on us. We would wait and see.

Paul and I were able to write letters to each other through his sister. Paul was teaching me how to use the law book, and somehow, I was learning.

No surprise, the federal government put a detainer on me for two bank burglaries in New Jersey. I knew that was coming.

Time was moving slowly. I was in Danville County for about two months. The first thing I did was go on a hunger strike. They fed us cold cereal for breakfast every morning I was there. I could not take it anymore. I told the guard, "I want a hot breakfast. I need some eggs and some ham and won't eat until we get some hot food for breakfast in this jail." He then asked if I was really going on a hunger strike. I said, "Yes," and he locked me back in my cell.

I knew the newspaper for this little town would have a field day with this story. I also knew all the other inmates felt the same way. The guard came by at lunch and dinnertime and asked me if I wanted to eat. I said, "No thanks." The first day felt slow, and I was so hungry I could have eaten a bear. The second day was a little harder. The guard was there for breakfast and asked if I was going to eat. I said, "No thank you. I want a hot breakfast," and he locked my cell and walked away. He did the same for lunch and dinner, and I said the same: "I want a hot breakfast."

I knew on the third day, either they would take me to the hospital, which was the law, or someone would talk to me. I was so hungry that I started to question my decision to go on strike. The guard was there at breakfast and asked me if I was going to eat. I said, "I want a hot breakfast and won't eat until I get one." He locked my cell and walked away. I knew by the end of this day, something had to happen.

Some of the other inmates wanted to do the same thing. I told them, "Just wait and see what happens." Well, right before lunch, the guard came to my cell and told me to get my shoes on. The warden wanted to talk to me. I got out of bed and put my shoes on, and the guard opened my cell and told me to walk to the main office at the front of the block. I said, "Okay," and walked to the main office. I was always respectful to the guards in this jail. I was a thinker, not a stinker.

Well, they opened the main office and took me to the warden's. He sat behind his desk and said, "Come in and have a seat." He asked me what was going on with me.

"I can't eat cold cereal anymore."

I was frank about needing some hot food for breakfast a few days a week. He then said that I should have put a request into him for hot breakfasts. I said, "You must know by now that we wanted a hot breakfast once or twice a week. Some of the inmates have been here for about a year, and they have not had a hot breakfast in all that time."

He sat back in his chair and told me to eat. He would take care of it. I said, "Thanks, I will eat," and he directed the guard to take me back to my cell and then provide me some food. As I was walking out of his office, he advised me to send him a request if I had any kind of problem.

"I will."

We got back to my cell, and the guard said, "You handled that well."

I told him thanks. He locked my cell door and walked away. About ten minutes later he came back with a ham sandwich, some chips, and some juice. That was the best damn ham sandwich I ever had. It was Wednesday. I would give them a week, and then if I didn't eat a hot breakfast, I would do the same thing again.

Well, we rolled out for Saturday breakfast and found some ham and eggs. I must say, that was a good breakfast. There were a lot of happy inmates in that little county jail. It made me incredibly proud that I could make a positive change for us inmates. The weeks went on.

The next thing I did was file a motion in the courts to separate my trial from Zeb, Danny, and Robert's. That way, they would get a fair hearing on this bullshit case they were charged with.

The courts granted my motion. That was my first win in court, and that made me very happy. The trial date was still not set.

The next thing I didn't like in the county jail was that you had to sign up to make a phone call, then wait a day to make it. You had to go to the front office, and they put a guard there who would put the phone on the counter while you called collect, and he could hear your conversation. I didn't like that, so I sent a request to the warden of the jail. I explained how this request was for payphones in the block, because the way he was doing it now was not efficient for the jail, and there might be a legal issue with the guard being able to hear our conversations with our families or our attorneys.

I wrote, "I hope to hear from you within the next few days." A few days later, I saw the phone company come into the block and install a payphone. Well, at that time, I knew I was helping the other inmates out as much as myself. I made a lot of friends in that jail, and I had a lot of respect from the other inmates. I must admit, the guards were cool, and the warden was a decent man. I had no problems with anyone there.

The next thing I did was put a motion in the courts that I needed law books, so I could fight my case with the feds. All jails have a law library, so each inmate can prepare their case. It was a law that inmates possess the right and the means to prepare their case. Once he found out about the motion, the warden sent for me. The guard took me to the warden's office, where he asked me to withdraw my proposal because the county was trying to find the money for a jail law library, and this might hamper the process. He also said I could use his personal law books in his office if I needed to work on my case.

I said, "That is fine with me," and I would withdraw my motion within the next few days. I also said, "I need to use your library within the next few days."

He said, "That would be fine." We said our goodbyes, and the guard took me back to my cell. I worked on a motion to withdraw my other motion, and a few days later, the new one was granted. After that, I was using the law library in the warden's office, and no doubt, I was using it a lot. I was working on my federal case almost every day. Time was going fast for me. I was trying to stay busy, and I was trying to help other inmates with their cases and work on my affairs at the same time. As the weeks went by, I was learning more about the law.

REWARD FOR ARRESTING OFFICER

I read the local paper and, on the front page, saw a story about the Pennsylvania House of Representatives honoring Danville patrolman Steve Bennick for his efforts in capturing Lucious Dale Johnson of Reading. *"Johnson was wanted by the FBI in connection with several bank burglaries. Johnson is awaiting trial on charges he tried to burglarize the Washington Fire Company in Danville this summer. Rep. Bob Belfanti Jr. presented Mr. Bennick with a copy of the resolution passed by the house."* Well, after reading that article, I figured I would spend the rest of my life in jail—not an uplifting way to start the day. But, life goes on.

ROBERT TURNS RAT

The next day, I got the news that Robert turned into a rat. I said before, I didn't trust him from the start. That was my feeling, and he proved me right. He told the cops in Reading that we did a house job in that town, and they sent a warrant and a detainer to Montour County Jail. Just another good day for me. Robert also told the Reading police that Zeb and Danny were in on this house burglary. Danny and I were in Danville County yet; Zeb was out on bail for Danville and the Reading charges. Zeb and Danny would take the Reading case to trial. The Reading prosecutor for this case would try to get them convicted first. Their attorneys asked for and were granted a separate trial. They thought that my background would hurt them if they went to trial with me. I told them that was an ace move.

Their trial date was set, and Robert was a no-show. He jumped bail, and the Reading police found out he was in Florida. So, they went to Florida, found him, and extradited him back to Reading, causing the trial date to be pushed back. After a few months, they got Robert, and it was time for Danny and Zeb to go to trial. A new trial date was set.

The sheriffs came, got Danny out of Danville County, and took him to Reading. They went through the process of picking a jury that day or so. Now, it was time to go to trial. Zeb said that he walked into the courtroom about ten minutes before the start, walked by Robert, and gave him the two finger guns, as if he were shooting Robert. Then, the judge walked in.

The prosecutor called Robert to the stand. He got seated, and the prosecutor asked him a question. Robert refused to answer. The prosecutor asked Robert if he was going to answer any questions, and he replied, "No." He would not answer any questions that were asked.

So, Zeb and Danny's attorneys asked the judge to drop all the charges against the two defendants in this trial. The judge asked the prosecutor if he had any other witness to call to the stand. The prosecutor told the judge, "No," so, at that time, the judge dropped all charges against Danny and Zeb. This was a bullshit case anyway.

About a week later, the Reading sheriffs came and took me to Berks County Jail. They would keep me there until the court date. The court date was a week away. That was meaningful to me; I could get some visits from my friends and family. I also knew some of the people that worked in that jail—that move was good for me.

Sandy came to see me, and so did my mother. I knew a lot of the inmates in that jail, also. This was a major week, but it happened so fast.

I was back in front of Judge Lieberman for a 1:00 p.m. hearing. I was in the basement of the courthouse until 4:00 p.m., when they took me up to the courtroom. While I was in front of the judge, he told me about Robert jumping bail, and that he had refused to testify last week. Ergo, he was going to drop all charges against me.

I said, "Thank you. Because the charges were not true."

He said that he believed me. Because if they were true, Robert would not have jumped bail, and he would be here to testify against me. He explained how Gil's testimony would not stand up in federal court, either, because he was not a credible witness. He made the sheriffs take me back to Montour County Jail.

I said, "Thank you very much," and he wished me good luck.

I was astounded. What had just happened to me? The case was dropped, and a judge just told me that Gil's testimony was bullshit. Gil was the only thing the FBI had on the bank burglary that I was charged with. This was one of the best days of my life. Judge Lieberman would always have a special place in my heart. He passed away a few years ago.

Mr. Lieberman, rest in peace.

The three-hour ride back to Montour County went fast. The sheriffs would not even talk to me. I guess they had concluded I was guilty no matter what happened. News travels quickly among the guards, and some of the inmates knew what had happened in Reading. They put me back in my cell, and I never heard anything about that case again.

GETTING SENTENCED

Well, a few weeks passed by, and it was time for sentencing for the attempted burglary on the fire company. I knew I would not take this to trial. They had caught me in the act of the crime. I would take a plea bargain if it was in the sentencing guidelines of the state.

In court, I was my own attorney, and the prosecutor came to me with a plea of one to seven years, to be served in Montour County Jail.

I told him I'd take the plea, but I could not believe what he had just told me. One to seven years in the county was an illegal sentence, because *your max could not exceed five years in county jail!* I was hoping they would give me this sentence. That way, I could appeal it as an illegal sentence and have it thrown out.

Well, they took me up in front of Judge Myers, and he sentenced me to one to seven years in Montour County Jail with credit for the time I had in the jail from the time of my arrest. The judge then asked me if I had anything to say.

I shook my head and said, "No."

Judge Myers then asked, "Is it easier not to explain?"

I said, "There is no explanation. I was wrong in doing what I did. That's all I have to say."

The judge went on, "You certainly know what it is like to be convicted of a crime. Is that going to be your profession? Are you going to be a professional convict?"

"No, sir. I don't plan on it."

After that, he wished me luck and asked the sheriffs to take me back to jail. I could not wait to go back to jail so that I could work on my appeal of this illegal sentence. I could not believe what was going on with my cases—the judge in Reading, and now this judge giving me an illegal sentence.

I got back to the county jail, pulled my law book out, and started working on this appeal. I was hoping the judge would overlook what he had done and not amend my sentence. I was working on my appeal for about a week. Then, one morning, I got out of bed, and around 10:00 a.m., the guard came to me and told me I was going to court and to get ready. I knew it. The judge had discovered his mistake. They took me into court, and the judge asked me if I knew why I was here. I told him I didn't know, but he knew I was not telling him the truth. I was not going to say to him that he gave me the wrong sentence, just in case there was something else happening.

He then divulged that he gave me the wrong sentence, and he was going to amend my sentence to one to five years, so I would be able to do my time in the county jail. He wished me good luck. I said thanks, and the guard took me back to jail, and he told me, "You're a very lucky man."

"I don't feel that lucky."

"The policies you changed in the jail help everyone out." I do not know to this day what he meant when he told me that. I know they helped out the inmates, but the guards? He took me back to jail and put me in my cell.

The appeal I was working on for the illegal sentencing was now worth nothing. Oh, well. I had about three months to do in Danville County. All I did was work on putting petitions in the federal courts. I put a request in that too much time had passed without action by the federal authorities; I also put a petition in that my constitutional rights had been violated because too much time had passed. I guess I submitted five petitions to the federal courts. Two, I had a chance to win, but I would have to wait and see what the courts said.

MAKING PAROLE TO THE BANK CHARGES

Well, the three months went by, and it was time to see the parole board. I knew that they would grant me parole because I had the federal charges to contend with and the max for that was 106 years. Sure enough, the board gave me a parole to the federal detainers.

Once I had my parole papers, they notified the federal authorities, and a week later, I was on my way to MCC, New York. I was glad to be going to a bigger jail. The Metropolitan Correctional Center was a high-rise jail in downtown Manhattan. They put me on the seventh floor, with two men to a room. The good thing was I didn't have to sit in quarantine because I had come from another jail.

MY NEW CELLMATE

They put me in a cell with Jeff R. He was in for doing the biggest armored car heist in the USA. They took over seventeen million dollars. He told me the reason they only took that much was that they could not throw any more bags of money in the truck. I had to smile at that one. I only wished that had happened to me. He then told me the story of how they drove out of the score with this truckload of money to this place where they were going to unload everything into another truck, and they could not get the armored car's back door open. They worked on it for hours and could not crack it until he found a button under the dashboard that opened the door.

He said, "I knew that the police were looking for the truck by now, and just after we got the money in the other truck and drove away, we passed a police car heading to the armored car!"

They all got away and split up the money, and after a few weeks, he started to buy cars and anything else he could think of.

After a few weeks of spending a lot of money around town, the FBI came to his home to ask where he got all this money. He told them he needed to talk to his attorney, and they arrested him. They went through his home and found 300,000 dollars. They brought him to MCC, and now he was my cellmate.

He asked me what I was in for.

"They believe I did two bank burglaries in New Jersey."

I didn't tell him anything about anything, about any other score I was involved in. I didn't trust anyone. The FBI would do anything to get me on other crimes.

Well, anyway, Jeff R. went to court and testified against his friends, and they were found not guilty. Jeff R. was the only one to get convicted of the armored car heist. They never got any of the money back, except what they got out of Jeff R.'s home. He did come to see me once he got out of jail. It was years later, when I was down in Virginia, supervising an environmental drilling site.

OTHER PEOPLE THAT I MET

This man from Pakistan was a drug smuggler. His name was Mena, and he was a very cool guy. We got along very well. He taught me how to feel cards. The deck of cards had to be new, and you could guess if the card on top was the two of hearts or any other card—you could just sense what they were. I didn't know what the cards were right away, but after a few weeks, I was getting better. Only by touch, I could tell you what the card was. Which shows you, I sat there for a few months, and nothing happened.

After the first month, I got a job in the kitchen, working in the bakeshop. After about three weeks, I was the head baker. I was making cookies, cakes, and cupcakes.

The guard that ran the kitchen was cool. After two months of working with him, he told me he would try to keep me there. I said, "That's cool."

I met a lot of people in that jail. This one guy, Frank C., became a real close friend. Mena, Frank, Jeff, and I would hang out all of the time. Frank would get the XXX adult books, Mena and Jeff would get the smokes, and I would bring the food. We had sex books, smokes, and food, and there was not much more we needed in that jail.

AFTERWORD

I want to thank all the readers for taking the time to read this book about my early years. I would also like to tell you that my story doesn't end here. The second book about my uncommon life as a safecracker will be coming out soon.

UNCOMMON
Life

Made in the USA
Monee, IL
03 February 2020

21262696R00132